SERIES ONE

PASTOR'S CORNER

ISAIAH O. ADIO

Copyright © 2021 Isaiah Adio

All rights reserved. No part of this publication may be reproduced, distributed, or transmitted in any form or by any means, including photocopying, recording, or other electronic or mechanical methods, without the prior written permission of the publisher, except in the case of brief quotations embodied in critical reviews and certain other noncommercial uses permitted by copyright law. For permission requests, write to the publisher, addressed "Attention: Book Rights and Permission," at the address below.

Published in the United States of America

ISBN: 978-1-953904-98-0 (SC)
ISBN: 978-1-955243-02-5 (Ebook)

Isaiah Adio
129 Kensington Blvd,
Blandon. PA 19510
Email: isaiahadio@gmail.com
www.pastorcorner.org

Order Information and Rights Permission:
Quantity sales. Special discounts might be available on quantity purchases by corporations, associations, and others. For details, contact the publisher at the address above.

For Book Rights Adaptation and other Rights Permission. Call us at toll-free 1-888-945-8513 or send us an email at admin@stellarliterary.com.

Dedicated to the Holy Spirit

Contents

Preface vi

Foundational Truth 7

    Chapter One: Your Best Is Yet To Come 8

    Chapter Two: Money Is Not Everything 15

    Chapter Three: Christ Love You Deeply 19

    Chapter Four: Remain Unstoppable 22

    Chapter Five: Goodness of GOD 26

    Chapter Six: GOD Cares For You 32

    Chapter Seven: Without Love, You Are Nothing 36

    Chapter Eight: Rapture Is Close 41

GOD Is Real 47

    Chapter Nine: The Ultimate Father 48

    Chapter Ten: GOD's Faithfulness Transcend Beyond Understanding ... 51

    Chapter Eleven: Believe in GOD and Jesus Christ 55

    Chapter Twelve: GOD Has A Plan For You 61

    Chapter Thirteen: Importance of Jesus' Resurrection 66

    Chapter Fourteen: GOD Shall Restore Everything You Have Lost 71

    Chapter Fifteen: Depend on GOD to Supply Your Needs 77

    Chapter Sixteen: The Mercy of GOD 82

Heaven Is Real 85

    Chapter Seventeen: Heaven Is Real 86

    Chapter Eighteen: Catching a glimpse of GOD's Glory 92

    Chapter Nineteen: Who Will Be in Heaven and What is Heaven Like? 97

Finishing Strong 103

    Chapter Twenty: Your Toiling and Pains Shall Be Over 104

    Chapter Twenty-One: NO Fear No Fall 110

    Chapter Twenty-Two: What You Started, You Must Finish It 115

    Chapter Twenty-Three: Finishing Well and Finishing Strong 118

    Chapter Twenty-Four: Protect Your Destiny 123

    Chapter Twenty-Five: Take Caution 131

    Chapter Twenty -Six: Remain Focus 138

    Chapter Twenty-Seven: Winning is Crucial 141

    Chapter Twenty-Eight: The Road To Victory 145

    Chapter Twenty-Nine: The Lord Shall Provide You With Strength To Overcome Temptation 152

    Chapter Thirty: Be Cheerful, GOD Shall Give You Permanent Victory 158

    Chapter Thirty-One: GOD Shall Deliver You From Shipwreck 161

    Chapter Thirty-Two: The Lord Shall Change Your Story 166

    Chapter Thirty-Three: Good Days Are Ahead of You 171

    Chapter Thirty-Four: You Are Taking Over in Jesus' Name 175

    Chapter Thirty-Five: GOD Is Able To Keep You From Falling 180

    Chapter Thirty-Six: Let GOD be your treasure 186

    Chapter Thirty-Seven: You Shall Rise Again 189

    Prayer Points 193

Acknowledgements 200

Preface

By Isaiah Adio

I waited upon the Lord for over ten good years to publish this book. The book is a compilation of my Sermons and Weekly Pastor's corners written at different times. It is made up of quotations, inspirations from the Holy Spirit, personal experience with GOD and excerpts from other references. I am excited because I know that your life will not remain the same after reading this book. This book cannot be substituted for the Bible. No matter how young or old you are or what your life has been like so far. I invite you to read this book. It is a wonderful resource of encouragement. There is a reason for everything. The ultimate goal is for the glory of GOD. You are part of GOD's creation and plan; you were made for GOD alone until you understand that there would never be peace. Each chapter points to the Lord Jesus Christ.

The book is organized into 4 parts (Foundational Truth, GOD Is Real, Heaven Is Real and Finish Strong) and 37 brief chapters. I have added bold to some quotes for emphasis. I strongly advise you not to rush it so that it would be impactful. Don't just read this book, take time to seriously consider what you have read and ponder on it.

My prayer as you read this book is that GOD will restore your potential fully, open your eyes to see the reality of Heaven and prepare you for a life in eternity.

FOUNDATIONAL TRUTH

Chapter One:
Your Best Is Yet To Come

"And God said, "Let there be light," and there was light."
- Genesis 1:3 (NIV)

With just one word, everything changed. On January 1, 2020, GOD told me that the month of March 2020 was very crucial in the agenda of GOD; it will redefine the existence of many individuals and many nations including the United States. It will give a new meaning to many lives. This was iterated to our church members many times in January 2020 before the COVID-19 pandemic. On March 11, 2020, the World Health Organization (WHO) declared the COVID-19 outbreak as a pandemic.

The situation with the COVID-19 pandemic will eventually pass away but people need to forsake their sins and truly seek GOD Almighty who is the omnipresent that holds everything in being. His power is ever-present in sustaining and governing all things. Recently, the Lord revealed to me that half of the world's population will relinquish, not in two days, but in a day if the people of the world are not listening to Him when the next event happens at GOD's timing. It would not be global warming or another pandemic, GOD revealed it to me, it will come in a form of gas radiation that turns people into a dark powder instantaneously. That's one of the reasons the Lord permits me to write this book to the world. But for the children of GOD, everything will change for better in Jesus' name.

The Bible says in Isaiah 8:18, NKJV – ***"Here am I and the children whom the Lord has given me! We are for signs and wonders in Israel From the Lord of hosts, Who dwells in Mount Zion."***

A true story was told of a Christian pilot who was flying at 30,000 feet when his plane exploded. Everyone in the plane was killed except him. As he was plummeting to the earth, he pulled the rip cord, but his chute failed to open. At the last minute, the chute did open but it was in shreds, hardly breaking the speed of his fall. Meanwhile, there was a Christian woman standing in her drive watching this horrifying scene. Knowing he was in desperate trouble, the woman prayed for his safe descent. The pilot was praying, too. He landed virtually at the feet of the woman. Looking up, they saw that the ropes of his parachute had caught in two trees, breaking his fall and lowering him gently to the ground.

That's a typical example of a miracle. I have good news for someone reading this book that the GOD I serve will be gracious to you, and you shall be for His signs and wonders as from now. Signs and wonders are considered impossible; they are miracles that are simply incredible, because they contradict man's normal experience.

"Men of Israel, hear these words: Jesus of Nazareth, a Man attested by God to you by miracles, wonders, and signs which God did through Him in your midst, as you yourselves also know"- Acts 2:22 (NKJV)

What are signs and wonders? A girl was asked in Sunday school. She stated they are true events that only GOD and His Son, Jesus could perform. Almost every miracle of our Lord was designed to meet a physical need. They were completed instantly and completely. They reveal GOD in action.

None of the signs and wonders takes place in a vacuum. None of them takes place, or is recounted, or claims significance, in and for itself. Their significance is only as actualization of the reality of a true Living GOD.

> *"And Joseph said to him, "This is the interpretation of it: The three branches are three days. Now within three days Pharaoh will lift up your head and restore you to your [a]place, and you will put Pharaoh's cup in his hand according to the former manner, when you were his butler. 14 But remember me when it is well with you, and please show kindness to me; make mention of me to Pharaoh, and get me out of this house." - Genesis 40: 12-14 (NKJV)*

Two full years had passed, and Joseph is still confined in Potiphar's prison, forgotten by the cupbearer of the Pharaoh despite Joseph's favorable interpretation and plea to be remembered after his predictions came to pass.

> *"And it came to pass at the end of two full years, that Pharaoh dreamed: and, behold, he stood by the river"- Genesis 41:1 (NKJV)*

The GOD the Father- all powerful, all knowing, all loving, and all wise can choose to work through means other than human instruments, and thus He spoke to Pharaoh in a dramatic dream.

> *"Then Pharaoh sent and called Joseph, and they brought him hastily out of the dungeon: and he shaved himself, and changed his raiment, and came in unto Pharaoh."- Genesis 41:14*

The king's frustration at having such impressive dreams and yet being unable to know the meaning was too similar to the experience of the cupbearer. Joseph was finally brought to the cupbearer's mind, and

Pharaoh was told of the unusual Hebrew slave with whom this official had spent time.

"For judgment is without mercy to the one who has shown no mercy. Mercy triumphs over judgment." – James 2:13 (NKJV)

GOD can employ various strategies and tactics to promote and lift someone higher. That's why I often called GOD- the Master Planner. Nowhere does the cupbearer mention the injustice of Joseph's imprisonment. The substance of the cupbearer's words to his master was that this young Hebrew slave was highly skilled in interpreting dreams.

"Then Pharaoh said to Joseph, 'Inasmuch as God has shown you all this, there is no one as discerning and wise as you. You shall be [a]over my house, and all my people shall be ruled according to your word; only in regard to the throne will I be greater than you.'"- Genesis 41: 39-40 (NKJV)

The best that Joseph could have dared to hope for was a release from his imprisonment. How far beyond this was his elevation to a position of power and prestige. Joseph woke-up as a prisoner and he slept as a second- in- command to Pharaoh. In another words, Joseph was promoted from pit to the palace. What could have taken politicians or any human beings many years to achieve. It took GOD a day to achieve. From now on, every lost hope and blessing shall be restored fully to you in the Mighty Name of Jesus.

It is possible to live in the United States with a population of about 300million or any part of the world, and be lonely. It's a lonely life when you are a good cook and there is nobody to eat the food you have cooked. It is a lonely life when you see something funny and there is nobody to share the laughter with you. It is lonely when couples living in the same house, but they don't talk to each other for days. It is a lonely life when you are promoted and there is nobody to celebrate with you. Beginning from today every form of loneliness in your life will be terminated by the Holy One of Israel.

The Bible says in Psalms 89:20-24, NKJV that *"have found My servant David; With My holy oil I have anointed him, With whom My hand shall be established; Also My arm shall strengthen him. The enemy shall not [a]outwit him, Nor the son of wickedness afflict him. I will beat down his foes before his face, And plague those who hate him. "But My faithfulness and My mercy shall be with him, And in My name his horn shall be exalted."*

The life of David, the anointed shepherd boy, confirms the truth that anointing can lead to higher ground. GOD's presence is His glory and His person; His anointing is His power. When we receive the anointing, we are, in a sense, rubbed with GOD's power, which means that He is not only upon us but within us. Simply put, the anointing is the manifestation and the result of His presence. Without GOD's glory, we can never have His power. At the same time, the power without the presence will destroy a person; it will become an enemy. So we must have the presence with the power. The glory is given as long as a person is faithful. The power is the gift we receive as a result of the glory of GOD. Thus, a person can lose the glory and keep the power; typical examples were the case of King Saul and Samson.

David was a brave young man, curious and talented musician who endured persecution after persecution. But the greatest single factor that catapulted him to greatness and success was the divine anointing on him. It was the turning point in David's life. The youngest and eighth of his father's sons, David was GOD's pick for the throne of Israel among all his grown siblings who seemed more deserving.

"Now He who establishes us with you in Christ and has anointed us is God, who also has sealed us and given us the Spirit in our hearts as a guarantee." – 2 Corinthians 1:21-22 (NKJV)

When you are genuinely anointed by GOD with His Spirit, it means GOD set his seal of ownership on you, as a result of this; your destiny of greatness is fixed. Let all hell come against you, they will not prevail, your greatness cannot be stopped or reversed.

The anointing of GOD gave David a sense of his destiny and that sense of destiny eventually pushed him to be at the right place at the right time. As a result, he became almost fearless in every challenges of life. The anointing taught him lessons with a lion and a bear. He used those lessons to defeat a giant called Goliath.

From today, my GOD shall anoint and take you out of the valley and to the mountain top in the name of Jesus. When a river flows, it never looks back. All your problems shall end today in the Mighty Name of Jesus. Never to occur again!

"The Lord has appeared [a]of old to me, saying: "Yes, I have loved you with an everlasting love; Therefore with lovingkindness I have drawn you."- Jeremiah 31:3 (NKJV)

There was a day, I was mediating on life in general and Holy Spirit spoke to me vividly, and said *"Jesus Christ asked me to tell you that I love you dearly"*. That makes a big difference to me that my Lord Jesus Christ loves me very much.

"But now, thus says the Lord, who created you, O Jacob, And He who formed you, O Israel: "Fear not, for I have redeemed you; I have called you by your name; You are Mine." - Isaiah 43:1 (NKJV)

GOD is not just a mighty ruler who looks down at earth and sees a bunch of nameless people running around. He knows each one of us by name. GOD knows our troubles and our happiness. He made each one of us special, and He wants to have a personal relationship with each of us daily. GOD loves you and He will never leave you. And best of all, He want you to come to Him as you are by believing in Jesus Christ as your

Lord and Savior so that all your sins can be wipe away and have eternal life. Receive the best today in Jesus' name. Amen.

Chapter Two:
Money Is Not Everything

"But those who desire to be rich fall into temptation and a snare, and into many foolish and harmful lusts which drown men in destruction and perdition. 10 For the love of money is a root of all kinds of evil, for which some have strayed from the faith in their greediness, and pierced themselves through with many sorrows."- 1 Timothy 6:9-10 (NKJV)

Someone once said, *"They say it's better to be poor and happy than rich and miserable. But couldn't something be worked out, such as being moderately wealthy and just a little moody"*. But most people say *"I could handle wealth, or at least I'd like to have it!"* It seems as if more money would solve a whole lot of our problems. But, people often forget that wealth can create a lot of problems as well.

There was a book written by an American author and Nobel Prize Winner in Literature, John Ernst Steinbeck. It is called The Pearl [Bantam Books]. It was the story of a poor pearl diver who dreams of finding the perfect pearl. One day he actually finds it. The rest of the story unfolds how his once tranquil life turns into a growing nightmare as everyone else desperately tries to take his treasure from him.

> *"And I say to you, make friends for yourselves by unrighteous [a]mammon, that when [b]you fail, they may receive you into an everlasting home."* – Luke 16:9 (NKJV)

The Bible does not tell us that wealth or money is evil, but rather that it is extremely dangerous when it falls into the hands of those who are prone to sin. Money or wealth is like a loaded gun, it can be extremely useful in certain situations, but must be utilized carefully, or you may hurt others and yourself.

Money or wealth is like fire. Fire is a beneficial tool if used properly and under control. If it is utilized carelessly or with evil intent, it can become a powerful force that destroys both property and life.

> ***"Then Jesus said to His disciples, "Assuredly, I say to you that it is hard for a rich man to enter the kingdom of heaven. And again I say to you, it is easier for a camel to go through the eye of a needle than for a rich man to enter the kingdom of God"*** - Mathew 19:23-24 (NKJV)

In the course of events, I spoke with a lady, she doesn't believe in the existence of GOD. Money or wealth is her god. Her goal is to make money regardless of the situation of her clients. She was unprincipled, greedy and she was not afraid to advised innocent people for the sake of her profit. To be rich without GOD is to be short-sighted in light of eternity.

The Bible is telling us that wealth is temporary and that judgment and eternity are ahead. So to pursue wealth to the neglect of pursuing GOD or to trust in wealth as the solution to your deepest needs is sheer folly. As Jesus Christ pointed in Luke 16:9, the god of money will fail someday but the reality of eternity cannot be avoided by anyone.

> ***"Come now, you rich, weep and howl for your miseries that are coming upon you! Your riches [a]are corrupted, and your garments are moth-eaten. Your gold and silver are corroded, and their corrosion will***

be a witness against you and will eat your flesh like fire. You have heaped up treasure in the last days."- James 5:1-3 (NKJV)

Gold and silver are not subject to literal rust. But the Bible is using irony to make a point in the above passage. When GOD brings judgment, even these precious metals will be doomed to corruption.

Saddam Hussein had an estimated net worth of $2 billion as of 2003. What good were all his money and wealth when a coalition of foreign nations led by the U.S. and the U.K. invaded Iraq and he was captured in a hole?

But death is the last resort for anyone. Late Senator John McCain was one of the most influential political voices for decades. He was a maverick and a fighter, never afraid to stand for his beliefs. He said, *"If I took offense at everybody who has said something about me, or disparaged me or something like that. Life is too short."* He was right. Life is short and eternity is real.

"But God said to him, 'Fool! This night your soul will be required of you; then whose will those things be which you have provided?'" – Luke 12:20 (NKJV)

As the rich fool in Jesus' parable found out, he had plenty stored up for this life, but when he died, he was poor where it mattered most; he was not rich toward GOD. To be rich without GOD gives temporary comfort and ease, but long-term misery. The ungodly rich mistakenly think that they are relieving themselves and their families from hardships through their wealth and possessions but they are storing up misery and hardship for the final judgment.

"But if anyone does not provide for his own, and especially for those of his household, he has denied the faith and is worse than an unbeliever." –1 Timothy 5:8 (NKJV)

The Bible commands us to provide the necessities of life for our families and ourselves. There is nothing wrong in being wealthy or rich. There is nothing wrong with living comfortably. We can do much more to serve the Lord when life is not a constant struggle just to survive.

Living in a good house, having good jobs, positions, automobiles, washing machines, dishwashers, lawnmowers, and even computer are good. These things become a problem when they begin to control us, instead of us controlling them. It is possible to enjoy the comforts of life without GOD, but if we fall into that, those comforts will become a snare.

> ***"For by grace you have been saved through faith, and that not of yourselves; it is the gift of God, not of works, lest anyone should boast."*** - Ephesians 2:8-9 (NKJV)

The Bible is clear that there are godly rich people and there are ungodly poor people. Salvation is by grace through faith in Jesus Christ the Son of GOD alone. Our responsibility is to be faithful to GOD in the realm of financial stewardship. You either trust in money or wealth that you now see or in the GOD that you will see one day. If you trust in GOD by accepting Jesus Christ as the Lord of your life, then you should be obedient to be a good steward of the money and possessions that He entrusts to you. He owns it all; we must give an account to Him of how we used it.

Chapter Three:
Christ Love You Deeply

"Eye has not seen, nor ear heard, Nor have entered into the heart of man The things which God has prepared for those who love Him." -1 Corinthians 2:9 (NKJV)

It is appropriate to remind you that what is in store for you in Heaven is far more than what you have seen, heard, or even imagined in this present world. After all, this world is corrupted as a result of sin. There is, on every side, distrust, discrimination, depression, discouragement, disbelief. As Jesus Himself predicted, there are **"wars and rumors of wars"**, and every day more news is written about threat of war with North Korea, Iran, election collusion, corruption, effects of climate change, drug abuse, gang activity, racism, terrorism and other human self-destructive ways.

We should constantly look forward to that day when our Heavenly Father, GOD shall wipe away all our tears, when we shall be welcomed home, when we shall experience ultimate peace and tranquility, when there shall be no more pain neither sorrow, nor crying, neither death nor sickness, no more bill nor taxes to be paid (Revelation 21:4, paraphrase).

GOD has reserved for us blessings which cannot be fully embraced by our five human senses nor even by our thought processes. GOD is greater than what we can see with our physical eyes at our present level (Exodus 33:20, paraphrase); therefore, anything He has held in reserve for us is also beyond our current ability to perceive or understand.

The Bible says in Romans 8:35-37, NIV that *"Who shall separate us from the love of Christ? Shall trouble or hardship or persecution or famine or nakedness or danger or sword? As it is written: "For your sake we face death all day long; we are considered as sheep to be slaughtered."* No, in all these things we are more than conquerors through him who loved us."

In another words, what can separate us from our love to Christ or His love to us. GOD expected our love for Christ to be so strong, that it will surmount and survive all opposition and all trials. There are people who are called *"summer friends"* because they desert us in the winter of adversity. But the love that Christ has for us can never be compared to anything and it is greatly exalted by the fact that, none of all possible adverse circumstances can ever changes His love for us. Christ loves us both in the summer and winter of life. He is the best friend you can ever count on. His love for us is through thick and thin. Christ love for us is far beyond sentiment, beyond charity, beyond friendship, beyond this life itself. Christ love is eternal and forever. One day, He is looking to host us to His banquet in Heaven.

The Bible says 1 Corinthians 13:12, NIV that *"For now we see only a reflection as in a mirror; then we shall see face to face. Now I know in part; then I shall know fully, even as I am fully known".* We should not presume to know better than GOD on how to run the events of our life. It is pride. Who are we to question GOD and say that we have a better plan than He does? We don't have the same wisdom and knowledge that GOD has, or the understanding of the big picture. We also are not privy to the perspective GOD has and should not claim to know better than He does what should happen and what should not. We should take GOD at His Word that He loves us and will bring us to that great expected end in every situation we find ourselves as we trust and obey Him in every steps of the way (Jeremiah 29:11, paraphrase).

My friend, are you willing to check on the status of your relationship with GOD? Are you among **"those who love GOD unconditionally"**? Are you among those who wait for and abide with Him? If the answer is yes, then the promise is yours.

Chapter Four: Remain Unstoppable

"I have found David my servant; with my sacred oil I have anointed him. My hand will sustain him; surely my arm will strengthen him. The enemy will not get the better of him; the wicked will not oppress him. I will crush his foes before him and strike down his adversaries. My faithful love will be with him, and through my name his horn[a] will be exalted."- Psalms 89:20-24 (NIV)

The life of David, the anointed shepherd boy, confirms the truth that anointing can lead to higher ground. GOD's presence is His glory and His person; His anointing is His power. When we receive the anointing, we are, in a sense, rubbed with GOD's power, which means that He is not only upon us but within us. Simply put, the anointing is the manifestation and the result of His presence. Without GOD's glory, we can never have His power. At the same time, the power without the presence will destroy a person; it will become an enemy. So we must have the presence with the power. The glory is given as long as a person is faithful. The power is the gift we receive as a result of the glory of GOD. Thus, a person can lose the glory and keep the power; typical examples were the cases of King Saul and Samson.

David was a brave young man, curious and talented musician who endured persecution after persecution. But the greatest single factor that catapulted him to greatness and success was the divine anointing on him. It was the turning point in David's life. The youngest and eighth of his father's sons, David was GOD's pick for the throne of Israel among all his grown siblings who seemed more deserving.

"Now it is God who makes both us and you stand firm in Christ. He anointed us, 22 set his seal of ownership on us, and put his Spirit in our hearts as a deposit, guaranteeing what is to come." - 2 Corinthians 1:21-22 (NIV)

When you are genuinely anointed by GOD with His Spirit, it means GOD set His seal of ownership on you, as a result of this; your destiny of greatness is fixed. Let all hell come against you, they will not prevail, your greatness cannot be stopped or reversed.

The anointing of GOD gave David a sense of his destiny and that sense of destiny eventually pushed him to be at the right place at the right time. As a result, he became almost fearless in every challenges of life. The anointing taught him lessons with a lion and a bear. He used those lessons to defeat a giant called Goliath.

The Bible says in Philippians 1: 6, NIV that *"being confident of this, that he who began a good work in you will carry it on to completion until the day of Christ Jesus."* As a believer, GOD will complete what he has started with you. So remain undaunted even if the enemy unleashes all his forces against you. Your unwavering in the face of all the spiritual attacks and harassment will be your personal testimony that you prevailed, so that the purposes of GOD for your life will be fulfilled.

Let me share this personal encounter with you. A few years ago, I went to a Mexican pizza store in the City of Reading, Pennsylvania as I was waiting for my order. I felt the presence of GOD powerfully on me. As I was trying to control myself, groaning in the spirit, the pizza man and other coworker pointed to my direction. I politely asked them if I can help them. The pizza men said they felt the presence of GOD in their store at the moment, and it was coming from my direction. And I told them that I am a minister of the gospel that GOD decided to pay me a visit, and they said, yes, we can all feel it. They were all amazed; probably that was their first encounter. Each time I visit this particular store, the owner give me free stuff since that time.

The anointing of GOD is tangible. It can be felt. Just as electricity is tangible, so is the power of GOD. To fear and to cower before the enemy is a sign that you either don't appreciate the unfailing and great power of GOD that has been unleashed into your life with His anointing or you are not anointed at all.

The Bible says in 2 Tim. 2:20-21, NKJV that *"But in a great house there are not only vessels of gold and silver, but also of wood and clay, some for honor and some for dishonor. Therefore if anyone cleanses himself from the latter, he will be a vessel for honor, [a]sanctified and useful for the Master, prepared for every good work."* So, what are some of the dishonorable things we must rid ourselves of to qualify for *"the Master's use"*? These are things which make believers *"dishonorable"* because they defile them:

"But among you there must not be even a hint of sexual immorality, or of any kind of impurity, or of greed, because these are improper for God's holy people." - Eph. 5:3 (NIV)

The question is, do you 'secretly' do some of dishonorable things while appearing saintly to the public? Are you in a secret amorous relationship? Do you pass crude jokes *"gossip"* behind your people's back? Do you secretly covet things belonging to someone else? Do you secretly dabble in some of the abominable things forbidden by GOD?

The Bible encouraged us to give no occasion for any of the dishonorable things as believers, much less actually do them. It does not befit our status; it's inappropriate and scandalous!

GOD wants you to succeed in every area of life but you must get rid of dishonorable things. With His Presence in your life, you can. The glory of GOD upon your life can open doors of opportunities and place you at the right place at the right time for His blessings. Even if you lack the necessary qualifications, His favor can propel you forward to your destiny. One day of favor can secure your future forever. Holy and righteous living is the key to walking in the unstoppable favor of GOD. You need to know that GOD's desire is to solve your impossible situations and circumstances and that He has already made provisions for us in Christ Jesus

I pray a wall of fire around you and your family from now. Wealth will be attracted to you and not subtracted from you. You are walking on top as the head and not beneath as the tail. You are, unstoppable; the anointing makes you, unstoppable. Go higher in the Mighty Name of Jesus' Name. Amen.

Chapter Five:
Goodness of GOD

"And the Lord said, "I will cause all my goodness to pass in front of you, and I will proclaim my name, the Lord, in your presence. I will have mercy on whom I will have mercy, and I will have compassion on whom I will have compassion." - Exodus 33:19 (NIV).

GOD's resources are there for us always. This blessing is ours. Believers are chosen by GOD, and we are chosen and blessed before we have done anything or have been anything for GOD. Our heavenly Father has engrafted us, through the blessing of adoption, to partake in His Kingdom inheritance. The great light of this truth is that GOD wants to bless us with every blessing available to us. Our thanks are due to GOD for the Kingdom blessings which are of course, higher, better, and more secure than earthly blessings.

The goodness of GOD is not only an attribute of GOD but a foundational truth everyone should embrace. GOD pronounced everything which He created to be good:

Genesis 1:4 (NIV) – "God saw that the light was good, so God separated the light from the darkness."

Genesis 1:10 (NIV) – "God called the dry ground "land" and the gathered waters he called "seas." God saw that it was good."

Genesis 1:18 (NIV)- "to preside over the day and the night, and to separate the light from the darkness. God saw that it was good."

1 Timothy 4:4 (NIV) –"For every creation of God is good and no food is to be rejected if it is received with thanksgiving."

The goodness of GOD may thus be viewed as one facet of His glorious nature, and character and also the overall summation of His nature and character. You cannot have goodness without GOD, just as you cannot have GOD without goodness. GOD alone is good. GOD does not withhold anything that is truly good from His children.

"For the Lord God is a sun and shield; the Lord bestows favor and honor; no good thing does he withhold from those whose walk is blameless."- Psalm 84:11 (NIV)

The goodness of GOD can only be revealed through the divine revelation of the Scriptures; we cannot recognize true goodness, for it cannot be understood apart from knowing GOD and seeing life from His perspective.

"Surely God is good to Israel, to those who are pure in heart."
- Psalm 73:1 (NIV)

The composer of Psalm 73 was Asaph, who happened to be chief of the musician under King David. Asaph describes a period in his life when he had serious spiritual struggles. His premise was the goodness of GOD, particularly His goodness to His own people. GOD's goodness would constantly be poured out upon those who are righteous. On the other hand, the unrighteous could expect many difficulties as we can see from Deuteronomy 28: 25, NIV below

"The Lord will cause you to be defeated before your enemies. You will come at them from one direction but flee from them in seven, and you will become a thing of horror to all the kingdoms on earth."

From Psalm 73: 1-15 (paraphrase), Asaph makes some very sweeping generalizations implying that all the wicked prosper and the righteous, which surely included him, suffer. He wrongly supposes the wicked are always healthy and wealthy and thinks none of the wicked experience the difficulties of life. Even in their death, they are spared from discomfort. He likewise thinks those who prosper are all arrogant, blaspheming GOD, daring Him to know or care about what the wicked are doing.

> ***"This is what the wicked are like— always free of care, they go on amassing wealth."*** - Psalm 73:12 (NIV).

There is some measure of truth in this. Some of the wealthy wicked would be just as Asaph has described them. But Asaph has overgeneralized, making it seem GOD blesses all the wicked and punishes all the righteous. The wicked flaunt their wickedness and are blessed. The righteous practice their righteousness and are punished for doing so. As far as Asaph is concerned, there is good reason to consider joining the wicked rather than fighting them.

> ***"But as for me, my feet had almost slipped; I had nearly lost my foothold."*** - Psalm 73:2

Asaph viewed life from a distorted human perspective. To him, the goodness of GOD meant health and wealth. But Asaph later admits, he was wrong.

> ***"till I entered the sanctuary of God; then I understood their final destiny"*** - Psalm 73:17

When Asaph came *"into the sanctuary of GOD,"* he was able to *"perceive their end"*. Now, Asaph viewed the prosperity of the wicked in the light of eternity rather than simply from the vantage point of time. Those who seemed to be doing so well in their wickedness Asaph now saw in great peril. Their feet were on a slippery place. In a short time, they would face the judgment of GOD sometime. Their payday for sin might not come in this life, but it would surely come in eternity.

> *"And we know that in all things God works for the good of those who love him, who[a] have been called according to his purpose."* - Romans 8:28 (NIV)

GOD's discipline and wrath are good. GOD's holiness is good. GOD's righteousness is good. GOD is good in His entirety. There is nothing about GOD that is not good. There is nothing GOD purposes for His children that are not good. GOD gives to His children only that which is good. And He withholds nothing good from us. GOD is good, and He is at work in our lives for good. Nothing which GOD creates, nothing which GOD accomplishes, is not good.

> *"For God was pleased to have all his fullness dwell in him, and through him to reconcile to himself all things, whether things on earth or things in heaven, by making peace through his blood, shed on the cross."* - Colossians 1:19-20 (NIV)

The goodness of GOD is evident in the gospel of Jesus Christ. GOD is good to all men in His common grace, showering blessings on the wicked and the righteous alike. But GOD is particularly good to those who believe in the gospel. The gospel is predicated on the truth that man is a sinner, deserving GOD's eternal wrath. This is the bad news of our sinful condition and the eternal wrath of GOD which it deserves. But the good news is that GOD in His goodness has made possible one way by which men may escape judgment, have their sins forgiven, and spend eternity in the blessed presence of GOD. That way is through Jesus

Christ, the Son of GOD who lived a perfect life, died on the cross of Calvary in the sinner's place, rose from the dead and ascended into heaven.

"Therefore, God exalted him to the highest place and gave him the name that is above every name, that at the name of Jesus every knee should bow, in heaven and on earth and under the earth" – Philippians 2: 9-10 (NIV)

"If you declare with your mouth, "Jesus is Lord," and believe in your heart that God raised him from the dead, you will be saved"- Romans 10:9 (NIV)

Nowhere is the goodness of GOD more evident than in the person of our Lord Jesus Christ. In His goodness, GOD provided a way for sinners to be forgiven and to be declared righteous. It is not by any good works which we do, but on the basis of the goodness of the Lord Jesus Christ. If you have never trusted in His saving work of Jesus Christ; I have words of exhortation for you:

"Taste and see that the Lord is good; blessed is the one who takes refuge in him" - Psalm 34: 8 (NIV)

With this offer of salvation by faith in Jesus Christ- the goodness of GOD is directed toward our repentance. If we reject the goodness of GOD in Christ, if we reject the gospel, then we bring upon ourselves the divine wrath of GOD.

"Or do you have contempt for the wealth of his kindness, forbearance, and patience, and yet do not know that God's kindness leads you to repentance?" – Romans 2:4 (NIV)

The devil always wants to change's human perspective of GOD. In Genesis 3: 1-5, the devil was able to persuade Eve to disobey GOD by eating the forbidden fruit.

> *""You will not certainly die," the serpent said to the woman. "For God knows that when you eat from it your eyes will be opened, and you will be like God, knowing good and evil."* – Genesis 3: 4-5 (NIV)

The goodness of GOD is a perspective from which we can and should view all of GOD's commands, including His prohibitions. It is apparent from what happened in Genesis Chapter 3 as a result of the eating of the forbidden fruit that GOD forbade that fruit for man's good. The prohibition was an expression of GOD's goodness. Eve did not understand why GOD forbade it, but knowing that GOD was good should have been enough. What a good GOD forbids must be evil, and what a good GOD commands must be good. We must know the truth found in the Word of GOD to avoid satan when he tempts us to change our perspective of GOD. He often does this by causing us to doubt GOD and His Word.

May the living GOD grant us the understanding of His truth, and grant us the grace to embrace this truth, so that it becomes the perspective from which we view all of the events of our lives.

Chapter Six:
GOD Cares For You

"When I consider your heavens, the work of your fingers, the moon and the stars, which you have set in place" - Psalm 8:3 (NIV).

As I meditated and considered the magnitude of the universe, I exclaimed in amazement, and then asked GOD, my daddy how do you do this? Our universe is very large, but there is still more to it than what you probably realize. For a more dramatic example, scientists made us understand that the atomic energy stored in the atoms of a 200-pound man is equal to 157,307 atomic bombs (the ones that were dropped on Hiroshima, Japan).

If there is that much atomic energy in a 200-pound man, imagine how much energy that would be needed to create the whole universe. Imagine how big the GOD who created all these is. I find it amazing that people actually have the boldness to say that they will boldly stand up to GOD in the eternity, or some people that even say there is no GOD. Obviously, they don't comprehend the GOD who created the Heaven and the universe and everything that's in it.

"Woe to those who quarrel with their Maker, those who are nothing but potsherds among the potsherds on the ground. Does the clay say

to the potter, 'What are you making?' Does your work say, 'The potter has no hands'?" – Isaiah 45:9 (NIV)

Just as our minds cannot comprehend the magnitude and complexity of the universe, it cannot comprehend the magnitude and complexity of GOD. Obviously, GOD is far greater and more powerful than the universe He created.

"The LORD wraps himself in light as with a garment; he stretches out the heavens like a tent"- Psalm 104:2 (NIV)

Even though this universe is incredibly staggering in size, it is probably just a dot in comparison to GOD's actual greatness and power. I cannot even begin to imagine how great, majestic, powerful, and awesome our GOD is.

"I praise you because I am fearfully and wonderfully made; your works are wonderful, I know that full well."- Psalm 139:14 (NIV)

We should not take GOD for granted. Instead, we should be humbled by the wisdom of GOD as evidenced in creation. Think about your own body as it normally functions:

An average heart pumps about 2.4 ounces (70 milliliters) of blood per beat of heart. If 72 beats occur per minute, then about 1.3 gallons (5 Liters) of blood is pumped per minute. About 1,900 gallons (7,200 Liters) of blood is pumped per day. This adds up to almost 700,000 gallons (2,628,000 Liters) of blood per year and about 48 million gallons (184,086,000 liters) by a lifespan of 70 years.

In one day, the blood travels a total of 19,000 km (12,000 miles)- that is four times the distance across the United States from coast to coast. If all arteries, veins, and capillaries of the human circulatory system were laid end to end, the total length would be 60,000 miles, or 100,000 km. That is nearly two and a half times around the Earth.

Without any doubt, GOD is incredible. GOD takes that which is small and insignificant and makes it great, while He makes the great small and insignificant.

"You have made them a little lower than the angels and crowned them with glory and honor. You made them rulers over the works of your hands; you put everything under their feet" – Psalm 8:5-6 (NIV)

It is amazing that He has taken a personal interest in our lives and also, has invited us to be His friend. We should respond to GOD's love with the praise that is due Him.

"Come, let us worship and bow down; let us kneel before the Lord our Maker" -Psalm 95:6 (NIV)

GOD put all things under Jesus Christ's feet when He raised Him from the dead and seated Him at His right hand. Likewise, GOD decided to put everything He created under our authority as we accept Jesus to be the Lord of our lives. Through Him we are partakers of GOD's inheritance.

"and giving joyful thanks to the Father, who has qualified you to share in the inheritance of his holy people in the kingdom of light."- Colossians 1:12 (NIV)

The Bible says in 2 Corinthians 4:6, NIV –"For God, who said, *"Let light shine out of darkness,"* made his light shine in our hearts to give us the light of the knowledge of God's glory displayed in the face of Christ.". This is about the greatness and mighty truth about GOD. It is one that demands more than assent; it necessitates action.

"Now the earth was formless and empty, darkness was over the surface of the deep, and the Spirit of God was hovering over the waters."- Genesis 1:2

The above passage reveals how GOD has taken chaos and fashioned it into cosmos—order and beauty. I cannot imagine living in this present world without the support of Jesus Christ, the Son of GOD. The same One Who turned chaos into cosmos can make your life anew.

Chapter Seven:
Without Love, You Are Nothing

"Love never fails. But where there are prophecies, they will cease; where there are tongues, they will be stilled; where there is knowledge, it will pass away."- 1 Corinthians 13: 8 (NIV).

Many people have asked me about the prophecy for the year. The only thing I indulge to say is that Jesus Christ is coming soon. The Rapture is imminent. Imagine how you would feel if you were told that you had only a few months to live. You might try to cram a lifetime into those last days. You might travel to places you have always wanted to see. You might do things for which you had never found the time before. It would not be difficult to understand why you would want to spend your last days indulging yourself.

"Owe no one anything, except to love one another, for the one who loves his neighbor has fulfilled the law."- Romans 13: 8 (KJV)

Apostle Paul proposed a radically different response to a similar type of deadline—one each and every genuine Christians must face today. The believers must be reminded that our time on this side of eternity is limited on each passing day because the day of the Lord's return is daily drawing nearer.

In the light of this reality, we are challenged as believers not to indulge ourselves, but to give ourselves sacrificially in serving others. We are to develop and continuously encourage a mindset that denies fleshly lusts and refuses to make provision for them. The mindset that casts off the evil attitudes and actions which characterized us before our salvation and which are typical of the unbelieving world in which we live.

The coming of our Lord should challenge us to do more than be preoccupied with it. The important thing is to be found faithful when our Lord returns. We are to watch, wait, and work until He comes, whenever that might be.

"Love must be sincere. Hate what is evil; cling to what is good. Be devoted to one another in love. Honor one another above yourselves." –
Romans 12: 9-10 (NIV)

Love is not only the motivation which inspires our actions; it is the principle by which our actions are governed. Loving GOD and loving men is therefore to be the outgrowth of salvation and of sound doctrine. Love subordinates self-interest in order to serve others. It seeks others' gain at our expense. Emotionally and personally speaking, it is difficult to love people that hate you but judgment should be left to GOD rather than taken into our own hands.

Positively, we must put on the Lord Jesus Christ. Negatively, we must make no provision for the flesh. When we put on the Lord Jesus Christ we will manifest Him through our lives. When we do so, we will manifest His love, a love for those who had offended Him and who were His enemies. Putting on Christ means depending on Christ to live His life, His grace, and His love through us by means of His Spirit. There is no human means for Christ-like living. GOD has provided for us that which we lack. We must simply walk in the Spirit, by faith.

On the negative side, we must make no provision for the lusts of the flesh. Love and lust are opposites. They are incompatible with each other. The world equates the two, so "making love" is satisfying the lusts of the flesh. But in a biblical sense, "making love" is living in love as the Word of GOD encourages us in Romans 12, 13 and 1 Corinthians 13. Satisfying our lusts is the opposite of living in love. Living in love requires that we present our bodies, with their lustful desires, as living sacrifices to GOD.

> *"Rather, clothe yourselves with the Lord Jesus Christ, and do not think about how to gratify the desires of the flesh."* - Romans 13:14 (NIV)

Love is greater than faith. Love is eternal while faith is temporal. Faith is necessary in this life. But when the perfect comes, when our Lord Jesus Christ returns or when we leave this world to live eternally in His presence, we will no longer need faith, for we shall see Him and experience all that He has promised. Our love for Him, however, will last for all eternity in His Presence.

> *"And now these three remain: faith, hope and love. But the greatest of these is love."* - 1 Corinthians 13:13 (NIV)

Smith Wigglesworth was a mighty man of faith. There was a time GOD told him to get up, and go across a town to pray for a woman who was sick. Smith Wigglesworth obeyed instantly. When he arrived at the home of this sick woman, someone told him that the woman has just died. Smith Wigglesworth then said, **"GOD sent him to pray for her. Whether she is dead or alive does not affect him. Smith Wigglesworth entered the room where the deceased was. He picked the dead body up out of the bed, and leaned her against the wall and shouted, "Live in Jesus' name"**. At once, the woman returned back to life.

The Bible says in 1 Corinthians 13: 2 (NIV) - *If I have the gift of prophecy and can fathom all mysteries and all knowledge, and if I have a*

faith that can move mountains, but do not have love, I am nothing.".
If I can raise dead like Smith Wigglesworth. If I have the bigger congregation than Yoido Full Gospel Church in Seoul, South Korea where on a normal day 200,000 will attend one of seven services along with another two or three hundred thousand watching them on TV in adjoining buildings or satellite branches. If I can speak in tongues with different heavenly languages more than anyone on the face of the earth. If I could be more generous than the most generous philanthropists like Berkshire Hathaway's Warren Buffett who transferred $31 billion in wealth to the Bill and Melinda Gates Foundation or a chemical manufacturing executive Jon Huntsman who gave $723 million in 2007 to find cure for cancer.... and have not Love, I am nothing. Love is the great commandment and one of the distinguishing marks of a child of GOD (Luke 6:27-36).

The Bible says in Romans 12: 9 (NIV)- *"Love must be sincere. Hate what is evil; cling to what is good".* A dream is really just a goal we think we can't achieve. Maybe you dream of starting a business or getting a college degree, or having a mega church. Big achievements are made by those who aim high, and then maybe a bit higher. Likewise, you can make up your mind today with a dream to love your enemies, and start with genuine prayers for those who hate you, those who have persecuted you unjustly, or your critics who have ulterior motives to make themselves look better by making you look bad. However, Jesus does not say to like what they are doing to you. Rather, we are called to aim and love our enemies. Biblical agape love requires that you are concerned about the welfare of even your enemies. This means that you will do things that will benefit and not harm them.

Herbert W. Armstrong wrote in his book -Seven Laws of Success (Pg. 13):

"...most people have no aim—they are merely the victims of circumstance. They never planned, purposefully, to be in the job or occupation in which they find themselves today. They do not live where they do by choice that is, because they planned it that way. They have merely been buffeted around by circumstance. They have allowed themselves to drift. They have made no effort to master and control circumstances".

The Bible says in Matthew 5:45, NIV *"that you may be children of your Father in heaven. He causes his sun to rise on the evil and the good, and sends rain on the righteous and the unrighteous."* You may be saying, *"wait a second, I am already a son or daughter of GOD."* Yes. It is true, if you have believed in Christ as your Savior, you are a son or daughter of GOD. The focus of this book is not on attaining a relationship with GOD, but rather on being a person who shares the characteristics of GOD. Like we will say of a son, *"Like father, like son"* or a daughter we say, *"She's the spitting' image of her mother. From now on, aim to be like GOD in love.*

Chapter Eight: Rapture Is Close

"Behold, I shew you a mystery; We shall not all sleep, but we shall all be changed." - 1 Corinthians 15:51 (NIV)

The Rapture is so close! It is so close. In the past, the Lord has revealed to me many times about the reality of Heaven. He has taken me to heaven once where I met the Saints that welcomed me to Heaven, they knew my name and when I looked at their faces I knew their names as well though I never met anyone of them on the face of earth. I can remember I said it with a loud voice and with joy that I made it home at last! In Heaven, I remembered who I am on this earth; I remembered my children and the congregation. I can remember that there is an entrance to the gate of Heaven, remembered the cool breeze of Heaven, the unexplained joy in heaven and I can remember that the Saints that I met at the entrance gate of Heaven told me that the Master Jesus has prepared a banquet for me and as I was walking from the gate to the banqueting then I woke up.

In the last few days of the year 2020, the Lord revealed to me the reality of Rapture, the Rapture took place and many were left behind. The most pathetic was that many children that were left behind were forced to take the mark of the beast 666 on their palms because without it they cannot survive. It was very tough especially for the Christians that were left behind to survive without receiving the mark of the beast 666 on their palms. My intention is to make this an inspirational book and encouragement for everyone. There should be no fear and dread. I hope it gives you a sense of excitement, reality, readiness and anticipation.

"in a flash, in the twinkling of an eye, at the last trumpet. For the trumpet will sound, the dead will be raised imperishable, and we will be changed." -1 Corinthians 15:52 (NIV).

The Bible clearly teaches that all believers in our Lord Jesus Christ, dead and alive, will instantaneously be caught up to meet the Lord in the clouds, in the air! Our mortal bodies will, *"in the twinkling of an eye,"* be changed! This mortal must put on immortality. This perishable will put on the imperishable. This dishonorable will be raised in glory! This weakness raised in power! The natural body will be raised by a spiritual body!

"But about that day or hour no one knows, not even the angels in heaven, nor the Son, but only the Father." - Mark 13:32 (NIV)

Americans have an insatiable appetite for weather forecast, a 2018 study by Pew Research Center showed that 70 percent of U.S. adults say weather information is important to their daily lives — more so than any other local news topic. I am predicting the season! I believe we are in the season of Jesus Christ's return! Do you think that GOD wants us today to be discerners of the signs of the times? Yes, I think so! The Bible in the Old Testament says

"from Issachar, men who understood the times and knew what Israel should do--200 chiefs, with all their relatives under their command"- 1 Chronicles 12:32 (NIV)

Having biblical discernment of what is going on is a great blessing. Hearing and seeing GOD's fingerprints and footprints all over the place is a great opportunity because many do not have this chance.

The Bible says in 1 Corinthians 15:50, NIV – ***"Now this I say, brethren, that flesh and blood cannot inherit the kingdom of God; neither doth corruption inherit incorruption."*** That is, we who are alive [flesh and blood] cannot go directly into heaven, in this form. We have to be changed first.

"For we must all appear before the judgment seat of Christ; that every one may receive the things done in his body, according to that he hath done, whether it be good or bad." - 2 Corinthians 5:10 (NIV)

The Second Coming of Christ has two phases to it: Before the 7-year tribulation, He removes his church from the earth. He rewards Christians for their faithful service to Him at the Bema seat of judgment, then the great feast called the banqueting table of the Lamb takes place.

"Seventy weeks are determined upon thy people and upon thy holy city, to finish the transgression, and to make an end of sins, and to make reconciliation for iniquity, and to bring in everlasting righteousness, and to seal up the vision and prophecy, and to anoint the most Holy." – Daniel 9:24 (NIV)

While the church is in a state of unimaginable joy, having face-to-face communion with the Lord and with one another, all hell will be breaking out on earth during the last 7 years of earth history called Daniel's 70th week or the 7-year period of tribulation described in Revelation 19.

"He is dressed in a robe dipped in blood, and his name is the Word of God. The armies of heaven were following him, riding on white horses and dressed in fine linen, white and clean." – Revelation 19:13-14 (NIV).

In the Rapture, Jesus Christ returns for His church, which meets him in the clouds, in the air. Only the church sees it. It happens in a split second. At the second coming, Christ returns with his glorified church to destroy Antichrist, the false prophet and their armies—and every eye sees it. And it takes place over a certain period of time. These are two separate events, separated by at least 7 years from each other.

The Bible says in Luke 21:25, NIV -**"There will be signs in the sun, moon and stars. On the earth, nations will be in anguish and perplexity at the roaring and tossing of the sea."** When the Lord revealed to me about the Rapture, I saw the sun and moon disappear and nineteen moons appear while Rapture took place.

"Then there came flashes of lightning, rumblings, peals of thunder and a severe earthquake. No earthquake like it has ever occurred since mankind has been on earth, so tremendous was the quake. The great city split into three parts, and the cities of the nations collapsed. God remembered Babylon the Great and gave her the cup filled with the wine of the fury of his wrath. Every island fled away and the mountains could not be found." – Revelations 16: 18-20 (NIV)

The final bowl of judgment of Revelation 16 is the world's greatest earthquake, which causes every mountain on earth to flatten. And every island disappears. Remember, islands are mountains in the sea. Can you imagine the Tsunamis that will cover the mainland? In other words, the air we breathe and the ground we stand on is less secure, less dependable than the word of GOD.

Therefore, I am inclined to believe that the Rapture of the church could very well be accompanied by some kind of natural catastrophe that will cause a great cloudy phenomenon to encompass the earth so that the disappearance of the church will be explained away naturalistically, rather than theologically. So that when the world sees that the church is gone, they will explain their disappearance naturalistically rather than recognizing this is the Rapture.

I do think there would be a great newscast all over the world saying the disappearance and the dropping out of some people in relation to the catastrophe.

> *"When these things begin to take place, stand up and lift up your heads, because your redemption is drawing near."* - Luke 21:28 (NIV)

The Rapture is imminent and it is so close. The saints that are upon the earth, who are alive, shall be quickened and be caught up to meet him. I am encouraging you to be on guard, so that your hearts will not be weighted down with this message but make the most of this present opportunity, whether in the form of witness, stewardship, or holy living. This is comforting because genuine believers shall be Raptured and delivered from the earth before the great Tribulation breaks upon this earth.

I am leaving you with Apostle Paul's exhortation in 1 Corinthians 15:58, NIV - *"Stand firm. Let nothing move you. Always give yourselves fully to the work of the Lord, because you know that your labor in the Lord is not in vain."*

GOD Is Real

Chapter Nine: The Ultimate Father

"Every good and perfect gift is from above, coming down from the Father of the heavenly lights, who does not change like shifting shadows."- James 1:17 (NIV)

The Bible reveals GOD as our LORD and calls Him *"Father"* in both Old and New Testaments. The GOD who is all-powerful is the same GOD who is good and wise; He is the Father of all, that's why you should commit to the LORD whatever you do, and your plans will succeed.

The goodness of GOD is a perspective from which we can and should view GOD as the ultimate Father.

1. Ephesians 3:15 (paraphrase) stated that every family under heaven is named or set aside for Him.

2. Psalms 68:5 (paraphrase) declared that GOD is the Father of the fatherless and protector of widows.

3. Psalm 10:14 (paraphrase) confirmed GOD as a loving Father- the helper of the fatherless.

> *"Though my father and mother forsake me, the Lord will receive me."*
> \- Psalm 27:10 (NIV)

The LORD GOD is more than willing to help make up for absent fathers. When my earthly father passed on to glory in 2010, I was so upset for many days, One day, GOD the Father came to console me, yet I refused to be consoled. I find it difficult to let go. GOD then asked me this question *"Am I not more than your earthly father"*. When I realized the tone of His voice, immediately my eyes opened wide with fear because I know the implication of upsetting my real Father which is GOD Almighty. The GOD that cannot die and at the same time He can never leave nor forsake me. He is more than enough for me.

Surely the most wonderful aspect of being a Christian is that we all have a unique relationship with the Creator of the universe, the GOD and Father of Jesus, the Living Spirit who is Lord of all history.

> *"For I have chosen him, so that he will direct his children and his household after him to keep the way of the Lord by doing what is right and just, so that the Lord will bring about for Abraham what he has promised him."* - Genesis 18:19 (NIV)

Abraham was chosen by GOD because of his character. He was not chosen because he was sinless or would live a sinless life after being chosen, but because he was the type of individual who would want to please GOD and raise his family with that same desire. Abraham was a leader of his family. *"He will direct his children and his household after him"* is a kind of statement which illustrates this quality. Abraham was obviously not afraid of his children. Instead of letting his children and household dictate the rules, he commanded them. How different from the modern's day fathers. Some fathers in today's society seem to be intimidated by their wife, sons and daughters. They are unsure of themselves and their authority; therefore, they make poor leaders and poor role models for their children.

Fathers, we are commanded by GOD to raise our children in the nurture and admonition of the Lord (Eph. 6:4). Our children are not to be left alone to raise themselves.

At the same time, fathers we need to love our sons and daughters unconditionally. This means life-long acceptance and an open door for the worst of prodigal sons and wayward daughters to come back home. It also means accepting and adjusting to the uniqueness of our children with different talents, capabilities and needs.

May GOD open our spiritual eyes to behold the wondrous things He has in store for us as father.

Chapter Ten:
GOD's Faithfulness Transcend Beyond Understanding

"And we know that all things work together for good for those who love God, who are called according to his purpose" - Romans 8:28 (NIV)

The faithfulness of GOD transcends beyond human understanding. To remain faithful to His Word, GOD can use everything He has created to fulfill His plans and to make His Words come to pass. Take for instance; GOD is morally just in using the wicked to achieve His purposes.

"Surely your wrath against mankind brings you praise, and the survivors of your wrath are restrained."- Psalm 76:10 (NIV)

GOD is righteous, and He is also sovereign. He is able to use the wicked, and even their wicked deeds to accomplish His purposes. In another words, any acts of wickedness against children of GOD cannot stop the plans of GOD for us. Those wicked acts against us will eventually prompt and catalyze us into the next level as long as we remain faithful to GOD and His callings in our lives.

For instance, the scripture says to King Pharaoh of Egypt:

"For this very purpose I have raised you up, that I may demonstrate my power in you, and that my name may be proclaimed in all the earth."- Romans 9:17 (NIV)

King Pharaoh's oppression of GOD's people, and his refusal to let GOD's people leave Egypt, became an occasion of blessing for the Israelite nation. It resulted in their release from slavery and their possession of the land of Canaan. Nevertheless, they did suffer under the hand of King Pharaoh and Egyptians for a number of years. GOD used the wicked to accomplish His purposes. GOD used King Pharaoh to bring Himself glory and to produce good for His people.

The Bible says in Habakkuk 1:13, NIV - *"Your eyes are too pure to look on evil; you cannot tolerate wrongdoing. Why then do you tolerate the treacherous? Why are you silent while the wicked swallow up those more righteous than themselves?"*

Prophet Habakkuk was accusing GOD of failing to do His job; he was demanding justice from GOD as a result of cruel violence against the innocent. Imagine you are walking down the street and you see a man being beaten by gangs of thugs. Then you notice two policemen on duty walking toward you and you drew their attention by shouting to these policemen, pointing to the man in distress. These policemen refuse to lift a finger to come to this man aid and just ignore you. Wouldn't you be angry with these policemen? This was how Prophet Habakkuk felt.

"Look at the nations and watch— and be utterly amazed. For I am going to do something in your days that you would not believe, even if you were told."- Habakkuk 1:5 (NIV)

Prophet Habakkuk thought that GOD had been asleep at the wheel, that He either did not know or did not care for His people. In our Christian walk with the Lord, at times, it might seem as if GOD has abandoned us, left us without any help and refuse to answer us.

Despite what we might be feeling during periods of spiritual loneliness, GOD's faithful presence with us is an unchanging and eternal reality. I want to let you know this today that we are never alone. Every circumstance we walk through and every emotion we feel can be viewed through the lens of GOD's truth:

"Be strong and courageous. Do not be afraid or terrified because of them, for the Lord your God goes with you; he will never leave you nor forsake you."- Deuteronomy 31:6 (NIV)

The problem is not that GOD is not doing nothing, but what GOD is doing is so beyond our grasp we might not even believe it if He revealed it to us.

"I am raising up the Babylonians, that ruthless and impetuous people, who sweep across the whole earth to seize dwellings not their own."- Habakkuk 1:6 (NIV)

Contrary to Prophet Habakkuk's perception, GOD was at work. GOD informed the prophet that He was raising up the Chaldeans to fulfill His plans. Chaldeans were arrogant, powerful, and wicked people, who loved to terrorize their victims. But GOD was raising the wicked to fulfill His purpose.

GOD is too powerful, too knowledgeable and He can use anyone or any situation to bring His intention to pass.

"You intended to harm me, but God intended it for good to accomplish what is now being done, the saving of many lives."- Genesis 50:20 (NIV)

I want you to know that in GOD's hands intended evil will eventually turn to good if we don't give up. For instance, for almost 20 years Joseph tied himself to the pillar of GOD's promise. He didn't forsake GOD in spite of hardship and pains. Eventually, his torn robe became a royal one, the pit turned to palace. The broken family grew old together. The very wicked acts orchestrated to stop his destiny and to destroy Joseph's life turned out to strengthen him and to fulfillment of his destiny.

> *"Yes, and from ancient days I am he. No one can deliver out of my hand. When I act, who can reverse it?".*- Isaiah 43:13 (NIV)

I love calling GOD, the Master Planner due to certain events in my life. Nothing escapes His reach. Both past, present and future are under GOD's control. GOD is sovereign, in complete control of all things, including every event in our lives. Nothing will happen that will catch GOD by surprise. Nothing happens that is outside His control.

GOD stretches the yarn and intertwines the colors. Every king, president, man or woman, despot, rich, galaxies, weather conditions, moon, heavens, earth, and molecule are at His command. He passes the shuttle back and forth across the generations, and as He does, a design emerges. I want you to know that whatever Satan has weaved in your life; GOD is ready to unweave today as you trust in His power and in the name of Jesus Christ the son of GOD.

> *"See, the enemy is puffed up; his desires are not upright—but the righteous person will live by his faithfulness."*- Habakkuk 2:4 (NIV)

Since we cannot anticipate how GOD will accomplish His purposes and promises, and since we most often cannot understand what GOD is doing since we are limited in knowing precisely, we are obligated to live by faith, if we are looking to Him for healing, deliverance, promotion, jobs, restoration or salvation.

Chapter Eleven:
Believe in GOD and Jesus Christ

"Do not let your hearts be troubled. You believe in God; believe also in me. My Father's house has many rooms; if that were not so, would I have told you that I am going there to prepare a place for you?" - John 14:1-2 (NIV)

After a few months of late nights at church to get our church building ready for a weekend church building dedication. The next day, Monday was busy day as usual, later in the evening I tried to mow the lawn at our residence, and visit a church family member. I realized that I needed some pain relievers to complete the set agenda.

After looking at some products, I noticed that virtually every advertisement for pain relievers claims the same thing—fast relief? I didn't see any advertisement that states: ***"Our product will not give you quick relief. If you purchase it and take the recommended dosage, nothing will happen for some time"***

"Thomas said to him, "Lord, we don't know where you are going, so how can we know the way?"- John 14:5 (NIV)

The immediate effect of our Lord's words to His disciples was confusion and sadness. I would like to suggest that this was exactly what our Lord intended them to produce—for the moment. The Lord Jesus Christ' words were not intended to produce *"fast relief,"* but eternal joy.

"Have faith in God," Jesus answered"- Mark 11:22 (NIV)

The disciples were told what will give their troubled hearts relief: faith—faith in GOD the Father and in GOD the Son.

"Jesus answered, "I am the way and the truth and the life. No one comes to the Father except through me."- John 14: 6 (NIV)

To have faith in the Son, Jesus means to trust Him. Simply fully without reservation.

When a person has faith in Jesus, it means that he or she believes who Jesus is (GOD in human form) and trusts what Jesus has done (died and resurrected). This faith in the person and work of Christ is what saves.

"Everyone who believes that Jesus is the Christ is born of God, and everyone who loves the father loves his child as well." – 1 John 5:1 (NIV)

Without faith in Jesus, we remain in sin and cannot be accepted into GOD's presence in Heaven. With faith in Jesus, we are given access to the Father as GOD's own children through the Lord Jesus Christ.

"Yet to all who did receive him, to those who believed in his name, he gave the right to become children of God" – John 1:12 (NIV)

The bad news for the disciples was that Jesus was going away without them. The good news puts all this into perspective. He is going to His Father's house; He is going back to Heaven. He is going there to prepare a place for His disciples (and all of us) so that we can be with Him for all eternity.

"My Father's house has many rooms; if that were not so, would I have told you that I am going there to prepare a place for you?" - John 14:2 (NIV)

You might be wondering, why is it taking Jesus so long to prepare this place for us? After all, doesn't the Father's house already have many dwelling places? Is Jesus taking up carpentry again, in heaven, and busily building rooms for us His children?" I think we know better than that. It only took seven days to create the Heavens and the earth, so why is it taking Him so long to make a place ready for us?

"And I heard a loud voice from the throne saying, "Look! God's dwelling place is now among the people, and he will dwell with them. They will be his people, and God himself will be with them and be their God. 'He will wipe every tear from their eyes. There will be no more death'[a] or mourning or crying or pain, for the old order of things has passed away." - Revelation 21:3-4 (NIV).

While on this earth, Jesus referred to the temple as His Father's house.

"To those who sold doves he said, "Get these out of here! Stop turning my Father's house into a market! - John 2:16 (NIV)

Now, it is apparent that He is speaking of His heavenly "home" and not the temple in Jerusalem or any place on this earth. In Heaven, there will be no temple, for GOD's place of dwelling will be with His saints.

"I did not see a temple in the city, because the Lord God Almighty and the Lamb are its temple. The city does not need the sun or the moon to shine on it, for the glory of God gives it light, and the Lamb is its lamp." - Revelation 21:22-23 (NIV)

GOD is delaying the outpouring of His wrath on guilty sinners, destined to condemnation, so that He might manifest His grace by saving those who are His objects of mercy.

"What if God, although choosing to show his wrath and make his power known, bore with great patience the objects of his wrath—prepared for destruction? What if he did this to make the riches of his glory known to the objects of his mercy, whom he prepared in advance for glory"- Romans 9:22-23 (NIV)

The punishment of guilty sinners is delayed until the full measures of those prepared for glory are saved. Thus, what our Lord is presently preparing—a holy temple, a congregation of believers in whom, and among whom, He will dwell for all eternity. When the disciples comprehend what Master Jesus is saying here, they will look on His absence in an entirely different light. It is better for them that He leaves them, for a time, so that they may dwell with Him for all eternity.

The Bible says in Mathew 16:19, NIV —" ***I will give you the keys of the kingdom of heaven; whatever you bind on earth will be bound in heaven, and whatever you loose on earth will be loosed in heaven.***".

Jesus is the life. We know that He has raised the dead to life. For instance, Jesus raised Lazarus from the dead, after he had been in the tomb four days! Jesus gives life, but this is because He is the source of life. He is the One who called Heaven and earth (and the church) into existence.

"The Son is the image of the invisible God, the firstborn over all creation. For in him all things were created: things in heaven and on earth, visible and invisible, whether thrones or powers or rulers or authorities; all things have been created through him and for him. He is before all things, and in him all things hold together. And he is the head of the body, the church; he is the beginning and the firstborn from among the dead, so that in everything he might have the supremacy. For God was pleased to have all his fullness dwell in him, and through him to reconcile to himself all things, whether things on earth or

things in heaven, by making peace through his blood, shed on the cross."- Colossians 1:15-20 (NIV)

To reject Him is to reject life and to choose death (John 5:21-40, paraphrase). Because He is the life, His life cannot be taken away from Him. He lays it down, just as He has authority to take it up again (John 10:17-18, paraphrase). To know Jesus is to know the GOD Almighty, His Father.

"No one has ever seen God, but the one and only Son, who is himself God and is in closest relationship with the Father, has made him known."- John 1:18 (NIV)

Jesus is the Word. He did not speak independently of the Father. He spoke the words which the Father gave Him to speak

"I have much to say in judgment of you. But he who sent me is trustworthy, and what I have heard from him I tell the world." – John 8:26 (NIV)

The world should believe Jesus' words because they are the words of the Father, the One that created the Heaven and the earth; they are the truth. But if this is too much, the world should believe His words because of His works. They are the Father's testimony that Jesus is the Son, and that He speaks for the Father.

"Very truly I tell you, whoever believes in me will do the works I have been doing, and they will do even greater things than these, because I am going to the Father."- John 14:12 (NIV).

These miraculous works which GOD has accomplished in Jesus Christ are not the greatest works that men will see. Those who believe in Jesus Christ as the Son of GOD and their Savior will do even greater works. The basis for these greater works is the Lord's presence and His promises to us. Once again, we see that it is better for Jesus to leaves us behind for a time until we see Him again in paradise, because His absence makes possible the *"greater works"* for us. Whatever we ask in His name, the Father will do in order to glorify Himself through the Son.

Jesus gave sight to a man born blind. He made the lame walk. He raised the dead. He healed all manners of sickness and diseases.

The purpose of the miracles our Lord promises is not the glorification of the men that GOD uses to accomplish them; the purpose is to bring glory to Himself and GOD.

He is not obliged to grant us every selfish request we might make.

"What causes fights and quarrels among you? Don't they come from your desires that battle within you? You desire but do not have, so you kill. You covet but you cannot get what you want, so you quarrel and fight. You do not have because you do not ask God. When you ask, you do not receive, because you ask with wrong motives, that you may spend what you get on your pleasures" - James 4:1-3 (NIV)

Jesus Christ is not encouraging His disciples to become miracle-workers here. He is urging us to believe His words, because they are the Father's words, and then every other thing shall be added unto us.

Chapter Twelve: God Has A Plan For You

"Look at the birds of the air, for they neither sow nor reap nor gather into barns; yet your heavenly Father feeds them. Are you not of more value than they?" - Matthew 6:26 (NIV)

Two birds were sitting on a branch of a tree. They were observing people rushing from one place to another. Both of these birds turn to each other, *"Why are people so full of worries and cares?"*. The other bird answered, *"May be they don't have a Heavenly Father like we do"*.

When we speak about GOD's promise to sustain and provide for man. It does not mean that man made a bargain with GOD on equal terms. It means that the whole initiative is with GOD; the term belongs to GOD and man cannot alter them in the slightest.

"But remember the Lord your God, for it is he who gives you the ability to produce wealth, and so confirms his covenant, which he swore to your ancestors, as it is today."- Deuteronomy 8:18 (NIV)

When GOD is about to bless someone or use someone, He will break that person because we all have a built-in propensity to trust in ourselves. The brokenness is the path to blessing.

"And the God of all grace, who called you to his eternal glory in Christ, after you have suffered a little while, will himself restore you and make you strong, firm and steadfast."- 1 Peter 5:10 (NIV)

The above Bible passage speaks about the way in which GOD likes to bring people to the very end of themselves before taking a hold of them and using them for His glory.

"Then the man said, "Your name will no longer be Jacob, but Israel, because you have struggled with God and with humans and have overcome." - Genesis 32:28 (NIV)

There was a man whom the Lord planned to make into a nation. How did GOD do it? He met Jacob one night and wrestled with him. GOD touched the hollow of Jacob's thigh and put it out of joint before He changed His name and called him *"Israel,"* means, *"a Prince of GOD."* The wrestling was to take all his strength out of him and when his strength was gone, then GOD called him a prince.

"David left Gath and escaped to the cave of Adullam. When his brothers and his father's household heard about it, they went down to him there. All those who were in distress or in debt or discontented gathered around him, and he became their commander. About four hundred men were with him."- 1 Samuel 22:1-2 (NIV)

When GOD was about to promote David to be King over all Israel. He had to escape to the cave of Adullam. He must go there and be an outlaw and an outcast, for that was the way by which he would be made king.

In another words, when GOD is going to give you an enlargement and bring you out to a larger sphere of service, or a higher platform of spiritual life, GOD might allow you to get thrown down.

"The Lord said, "I have indeed seen the misery of my people in Egypt. I have heard them crying out because of their slave drivers, and I am concerned about their suffering." - Exodus 3:7 (NIV)

That is His usual way of working. He makes you hungry before He feeds you. He strips you before He robes you. He makes nothing of you before He makes something of you. This was the way with David. He was to be King over all Israel, but He must go to the throne by the way of the cave.

Our GOD love names. One of His names is GOD El Roi—the GOD who sees.

GOD sees you where you are and He cares for you as you are. GOD sees our mistakes and yet treats them with mercy. GOD sees our sufferings, He sees whatever you are going through and in His appointed time He has plans to bring them to an end. We may sometimes feel that GOD is unconcerned about us, but He is faithful and always hears and sees.

"The righteous person may have many troubles, but the LORD delivers him from them all" - Psalm 34:19 (NIV)

I love GOD so much that's why I called Him my daddy. I know He first love me, He loves me very dearly too. GOD will utilize every tool within His disposal to bring every affliction to end. For instance, GOD utilized plagues to bring the misery of His people to an end after 400 years in the land of Egypt.

The Bible says in Psalm 66:10-12, NIV -" **For you, God, tested us; you refined us like silver. You brought us into prison and laid burdens on our backs. You let people ride over our heads; we went through fire and water, but you brought us to a place of abundance**".

Every affliction we suffer is an investment GOD is making in us. For instance, when parents send a child to college, it requires a great investment. And that parents hopes their child will apply himself to the rigors of his training. Why? Do they hope the child will graduate, come home, hang his diploma on the wall, then sit around the house watching television? No! Those parents hope their child will make his investment pay off by starting a good career.

> ***"For he does not willingly bring affliction or grief to anyone"*** *- Lamentation 3:33 (NIV)*

So it is with the Lord and our afflictions. Everything you go through as a Christian is a training exercise, behind which GOD has a divine purpose. He did not save you to allow you to cruise into paradise on a luxury liner. He saved you to prepare you to be used in His kingdom. The moment you were born again, He enrolled you in his school of suffering. And every affliction, every trial, is another lesson in the curriculum.

The Bible says in Luke 18:22, NIV -" When Jesus heard this, he said to him, **"You still lack one thing. Sell everything you have and give to the poor, and you will have treasure in heaven. Then come, follow me."**

To follow Christ, you must forsake all for Him, but you get blessings for time and eternity, along with trials in this life. For the rich young ruler in the above text, his gold had become his god. It was his idol, and he had to let it go in order to trust in Christ for eternal life. The love of the things of this world is an idol for many who profess to know Christ. We are like those things. We spend our lives collecting things. We accumulate so much stuff that we have to build bigger garages to store it in. But in light of eternity, no earthly possession will really matter.

> *"and envy; drunkenness, orgies, and the like. I warn you, as I did before, that those who live like this will not inherit the kingdom of God."*
> -Galatians 5:21 (NIV).

Jealousy, un-forgiveness, sexual immorality, selfish quarrels, bitterness, anger, self-centeredness. Apostle Paul lists the deeds of the flesh and then warns, we cannot cling to known sin and claim to be following Christ at the same time. He demands our exclusive commitment.

"But seek first his kingdom and his righteousness, and all these things will be given to you as well."- Matthew 6:33 (NIV)

Seeking first His kingdom means committing yourself to whatever GOD wants you to do with your life. Have you given Him all?

"Take delight in the Lord, and he will give you the desires of your heart."- Psalm 37:4 (NIV)

If you delight yourself in the Lord, He will give you the desires of your heart. Sometimes He grants your desires. At other times, He changes your desires to match His desires. But, you can trust the loving Father to do what is best when you give yourself fully to His cause. The plan of GOD for your life shall be fulfilled as you totally commit yourself to Him in Jesus' name. Amen.

Chapter Thirteen:
Importance of Jesus' Resurrection

"Since we have now been justified by his blood, how much more shall we be saved from God's wrath through him! For if, while we were God's enemies, we were reconciled to him through the death of his Son, how much more, having been reconciled, shall we be saved through his life!"- Romans 5:9-10 (NIV)

There was a time; I was at the Philadelphia Airport en route to Chicago for our Church Festival of Life. At the gift stores, many good sized selections of cards display were entirely secular. They ranged from **"thinking of you at Easter"** variety to the ones which had pictures of fuzzy teddy bears, bunny and Easter eggs, and some kind of inane holiday greeting. Thank GOD spring is here at last; somehow Easter is associated with the arrival of spring season.

If the greeting card displays of most stores are like the one I visited, we would have to agree that the resurrection of Christ is not considered very significant in our society. Easter bunnies and eggs have won hands down over Jesus Christ, the Cross of Calvary, and the empty tomb.

The significance of Easter is often overlooked or distorted by churches in America. All too often, Easter Sunday is more of a part of the celebration of the commencement of spring, than it is an observance and celebration of the resurrection of our Lord.

"For what I received I passed on to you as of first importance[a]: that Christ died for our sins according to the Scriptures"- 1 Corinthians 15:3 (NIV)

The death of our Lord alone would not have sufficed, since it is by our identification with Him in His death, burial, and resurrection that we are saved. Much more then, having now been justified by His blood, we shall be saved from the wrath of GOD through Jesus Christ. For if while we were enemies, we were reconciled to GOD through the death of His Son, much more, having been reconciled, we shall be saved by His life.

"By faith Abraham, when God tested him, offered Isaac as a sacrifice. He who had embraced the promises was about to sacrifice his one and only son, even though God had said to him, "It is through Isaac that your offspring will be reckoned."[a] Abraham reasoned that God could even raise the dead, and so in a manner of speaking he did receive Isaac back from death." - Hebrews 11:17-19 (NIV)

We can see from the above text that the faith of Abraham was a resurrection faith. So, too, our faith as Christians must be a resurrection faith. Jesus Christ says:

"Jesus said to her, "I am the resurrection and the life. The one who believes in me will live even if he dies, and the one who lives and believes in me will never die. Do you believe this?"" - John 11:25-26 (NIV)

Personal faith in the resurrection of Jesus Christ is therefore necessary because it is a vital element in a faith that leads to our deliverance from the eternal damnation in hell fire, and result to our salvation.

"If you declare with your mouth, "Jesus is Lord," and believe in your heart that God raised him from the dead, you will be saved."- Romans 10:9 (NIV)

The resurrection of Christ is not just a matter of fact, which should be taken lightly; it is literally a matter of eternal life or death. The resurrection is not simply a fact to be believed or rejected; it is a fact to which our response will determine our eternal destiny. The resurrection of our Lord was a kind of watershed event in the history of mankind. It was an event which brought about some significant, but seldom considered changes.

"Multitudes who sleep in the dust of the earth will awake: some to everlasting life, others to shame and everlasting contempt."- Daniel 12:2 (NIV).

The resurrection of our Lord assures all men, saved or unsaved, of being resurrected from the grave, but it in no way assures all men of experiencing the same blessings or destination after leaving this world.

"If anyone's name was not found written in the book of life, that person was thrown into the lake of fire."- Revelation 20:15 (NIV)

While the purpose of our Jesus Lord's first coming was not to judge, so much as to be judged, the purpose of His second coming will be to judge all those who have rejected Him, and who have sought to establish themselves with GOD on the basis of their good works or self-righteousness, rather than on the basis of Jesus' death on the cross of Calvary, burial, and resurrection.

"Do not be amazed at this, for a time is coming when all who are in their graves will hear his voice and come out—those who have done what is good will rise to live, and those who have done what is evil will rise to be condemned" - John 5:28-29 (NIV)

The resurrection of our Lord means that the sacrifice for sinners has been paid, once and for all, by our Lord Jesus Christ, and that this sacrifice has been accepted. Those who would persist in their sins, and who would not cast themselves on Christ for salvation must look for Him to return as a righteous judge, who will judge all unbelievers. To reject the Lord Jesus as the Savior is to expect Him as Judge. The resurrection of our Lord from the dead should not bring comfort, but dread, to the hearts of all unbelievers or those who have not accepted Jesus Christ as Lord and Savior.

> *"About three in the afternoon Jesus cried out in a loud voice, "Eli, Eli,[a] lema sabachthani?"* (which means *"My God, my God, why have you forsaken me?"* - Matthew 27:46 (NIV)

At Calvary, Jesus Christ bore the sins of the whole world. Jesus became sin for us and therefore the Holy GOD had to forsake Him temporary because GOD cannot stand sin. Jesus Christ shouldered the salvation of mankind. He trusted His Father step by step all the way to this defining moment on the cross.

Jesus Christ did not die for His sins, but for the sins of all, then we must first acknowledge that we are sinners, and that it was our sins that He bore on the cross. In other words, my sins and your sins put Jesus Christ on the cross so that He can join us to His Heavenly Father.

The greatest problem we face is not accepting the resurrection of Christ, and the fact that Jesus Christ lives forevermore. The greatest problem we face as sinners is not recognizing the fact that we are dead in our transgressions and sins, and are eternally lost without His death on the Cross of Calvary.

Just like in Biological Science, chromosomal crossover (or crossing over) is the exchange of genetic material between homologous chromosomes that results in recombinant chromosomes. Crossing over also accounts for genetic variation, because due to the swapping of genetic material during crossing over. Chromosomal crossover eventually matches chromosomes that break, and then reconnect to the other chromo-some. At this point, it is Cross-Like, and which eventually form DNA molecule the carrier of fundamental and distinctive character of human being. Those DNA molecules uphold our body.

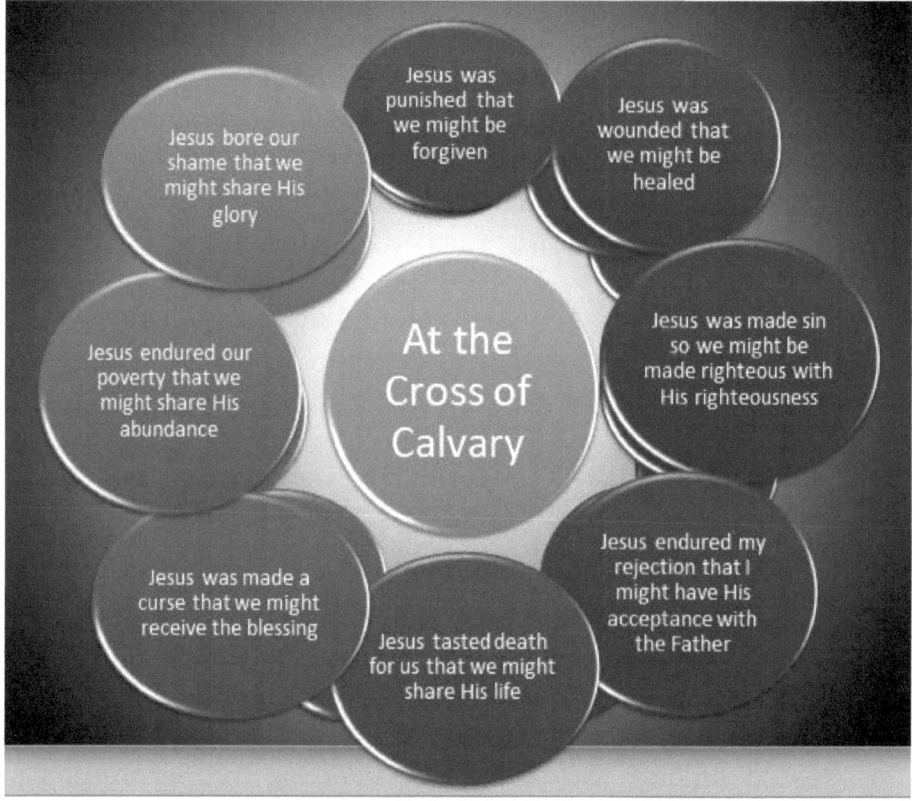

Likewise, spiritual chromosomal crossover happened at Calvary in which Jesus Christ divinely exchange our sins with His righteousness so that when our Heavenly Father see us as believers, He sees Christ righteousness and His blood in us instead of our sins. In another words, Jesus Christ through His death on the Cross of Calvary provides you and me with the DNA to uphold our lives.

Today, delight in the resurrection joy of Christ, celebrate it with your family, and treasure it until we get to eternity with Him.

Chapter Fourteen:
God Shall Restore Everything You Have Lost

"As one of them was cutting down a tree, the iron axhead fell into the water. "Oh no, my lord!" he cried out. "It was borrowed!"- 2 Kings 6:5 (NIV)

There is no feeling much worse than to know that you've lost something irreplaceable. In January 2004, my family moved from New Jersey to Pennsylvania to purchase our first home. For several months, we were going back to New Jersey to do our shopping, and to attend church service until we found our footings in Pennsylvania. One day, we were driving back from New Jersey when I realized that my wallet had slipped out. I lost my wallet where I had my bank cards, driver's license, and some other important information. It was a miserable evening that Saturday.

The above text contains the story about something that was lost and recovered. One can't be certain where the sons of the prophets were living at the time, but wherever it was, their accommodations were too small. Some of the prophets felt this would be the time to build a bigger facility, and at the same time, change their location. Prophet Elisha was asked for his permission, and he approved the plan.

> *"Then one of them said, "Won't you please come with your servants?"*
> *"I will,"* Elisha replied."- 2 Kings 6:3 (NIV)

The prophets were not content merely to have Elisha's permission to build in another location. They wanted Elisha to be present with them as they went about the task of building a meeting place.

> *" Then Moses said to him, "If your Presence does not go with us, do not send us up from here."*- Exodus 33:15 (NIV)

As I considered this request of Elisha, I was reminded of Moses' persistence in obtaining GOD's assurance that He would be with His people as they made their way from Mount Sinai to the Promised Land. Now, GOD's presence was somehow associated with genuine servants of GOD, His prophets, and especially with Elisha. They recognized and reverence GOD and to the things that represent His person and presence. No wonder they wanted Elisha to be with them as they went about this task.

> *"But I tell you the truth, it is to your advantage that I am going away. For if I do not go away, the Advocate will not come to you, but if I go, I will send him to you."*- John 16:7 (NIV)

How little do we grasp the privilege we have of His constant presence with us and in us, through His Holy Spirit that abide with us each day.

> *"The man of God asked, "Where did it fall?"* When he showed him the place, Elisha cut a stick and threw it there, and made the iron float." - 2 Kings 6:6 (NIV)

Elisha was with the prophet when the borrowed axe head flies off into the waters of Jordan. He hears the plea of the prophet and comes to his aid. He cuts off a limb and thrusts it into the water near the place where the axe head went in. The iron axe head floats to the surface, and Elisha instructs the prophet to snatch it out of the water.

I believe what happened here was a great intervention of GOD that results in a miracle. Some individual seem to find it necessary to understand how and why the axe head floated to the surface before they can believe that it did so. I choose to believe that it did so, assuming that GOD was not required to follow the laws of nature that He has set down.

"Jesus looked at them and said, 'With man this is impossible, but with God all things are possible'" -Matthew 19:26 (NIV)

Today, the reality is that GOD can work through ALL things which means He is not limited by any circumstances, human being or earthly government. GOD is not limited by time and space, when He comes to the scene ALL things must obey Him.

The Bible says in John 11:25, NIV- *"Jesus said to her, "I am the resurrection and the life. The one who believes in me will live, even though they die"*. Lazarus was buried in a cave, with a stone covering the opening. The raising of Lazarus almost looks like a dress rehearsal for the resurrection of our Lord Jesus Christ in the near future. Jesus orders the stone to be rolled away. We aren't sure who Jesus orders to move the stone. It could be the disciples, of course, but it may just as well be others, such as some of those who have come to mourn with Mary. I am inclined to think that Jesus deliberately employed those other than His disciples to remove the stone. Doing this would seem to require some measure of faith on their part.

"Take away the stone," he said. *"But, Lord,"* said Martha, the sister of the dead man, *"by this time there is a bad odor, for he has been there four days"*- John 11:39 (NIV)

It was Martha, however, who objected to our Lord's instruction to remove the stone. She protested that too much time has passed. The body will certainly smell badly, she explains. But beyond this, it just seems to reopen a very painful wound. It seems quite obvious that Martha was not expecting Jesus to perform any miracle here, and certainly not the raising of one who has been dead for several days.

> *"Then Jesus said, "Did I not tell you that if you believe, you will see the glory of God?"*- John 11:40 (NIV)

I certainly believe that GOD has purpose for everything He does. Everything that happens to us is for a reason, not just by happenstance or by random chance. At this point, Jesus Christ was trying to stretch Martha's faith and goal for the thing GOD had proposed to do. At times, GOD stretch us so that we can hold more of His power, gain more of His wisdom, more of His character, and to see and gain more of Him. GOD always wants to increase our influence and enlarge our territory.

> *"Then he touched their eyes and said, "According to your faith let it be done to you."* - Matthew 9:29 (NIV)

If we set a big goal, GOD will work in a big way. If we set a medium-size goal, GOD will work in a medium way. If we set a small goal, GOD will work in a small way.

> *"I knew that you always hear me, but I said this for the benefit of the people standing here, that they may believe that you sent me."*- John 11:42 (NIV)

Our Lord Jesus Christ was consistently claiming that He does His Father - the GOD Almighty's work, and that He works with GOD. The above prayer was intended to demonstrate that the miraculous raising of Lazarus was something that the Father does through the Son. This prayer does not specifically petition the Father to raise Lazarus. Jesus does thank His Father because He hears His prayers.

> *"When he had said this, Jesus called in a loud voice, "Lazarus, come out!"*- John 11:43 (NIV)

If our Lord Jesus Christ had not specified *"Lazarus"* every dead body in the whole region would have arisen from the dead. In shouting with a loud voice, Jesus reveals His confidence that the Father will hear Him, and that Lazarus will rise from the dead. Lazarus emerged from the dead with his burial attire. Jesus demonstrated that He is the resurrection and life the only one that hold the keys of death and hades (Revelation 1:18). No situation is too difficult for GOD to restore. He can restore back to life.

The Bible says in 1 Thessalonians 5:23, NIV - ***"May God himself, the God of peace, sanctify you through and through. May your whole spirit, soul and body be kept blameless at the coming of our Lord Jesus Christ"***. Stop and think about that for a moment. It's a serious question. Picture the way Lazarus was restored back to life. That's the way GOD desire to restore every goods thing that enemies have stolen in our lives.

GOD desires us to be preserved, sound, complete and fulfill His purpose in our lives. In another words, GOD's perfect will for us is to be whole, undamaged and intact in spirit, soul, and body before we see Jesus Christ.

In view of this, what changes would you need GOD to make for His perfect will to be fulfilled in your life and what would it take for you to be whole? GOD has as many miracles as you need. He is the GOD of miracles. GOD specializes in birthing miracles.

There was a time, I was passionately listening to a message from my father in the Lord, the General Overseer of our Church, Pastor E.A. Adeboye that a man who was very small in stature probably due to disease or DNA abnormality attended one of his crusades in Africa and grew taller within seconds. Naturally, his DNA had patterned his body to be very small. But that's not his heavenly DNA.

GOD is so great, mighty, powerful, glorious and wise that He has no limits and He can reverse the irreversible in a second. He can restore what has been lost. GOD has the master plan and original entry in His book which says that everything was perfect (Genesis 1:31). Some of us are Black, some of us are White, some of us are Latinos but in GOD's sight we are all one. Now, He's waiting for somebody to agree with Him and believe for His will to be done to make imperfection to be perfect.

"But I will restore you to health and heal your wounds, 'declares the Lord, 'because you are called an outcast, Zion for whom no one cares.."- Jeremiah 30:17 (NIV)

I am telling you today that your miracle is never too late. Have faith in the Word of GOD, speak and release it without wavering. There was another testimony to prove that your miracle is never too late. There was a Pentecostal Minister in Africa. This minister's father was desperately sick. In fact his father's death was so imminent that the doctor who came to see him went ahead and filled out his death certificate. After the doctor left, the church members gathered together to pray and while they were praying, he was healed. Do you know what the man that was sick did? He got up, took a shower, drank a cup of drink and then walked to the doctor's house to return his death certificate that was issued to him.

Clearly, GOD can never fail; it is never too late for a miracle. I am here to tell you today that GOD has one for you too. Believe in GOD's Word and start expecting the impossible!

Chapter Fifteen: Depend on GOD to Supply Your Needs

"Are not two sparrows sold for a penny? Yet not one of them will fall to the ground outside your Father's care. And even the very hairs of your head are all numbered. So don't be afraid; you are worth more than many sparrows."- Matthew 10:29-31(NIV)

Our needs are never unknown to the Lord GOD Almighty; GOD is the truly transcendent Being. GOD created all things on the earth, beneath the earth and in the heavens above, yet He exists above and independent from them. All things are upheld by His mighty power, yet He is upheld by Himself alone. The whole universe exists in Him and for Him that He may receive all glory, honor, praise and power.

"The Son is the radiance of God's glory and the exact representation of his being, sustaining all things by his powerful word. After he had provided purification for sins, he sat down at the right hand of the Majesty in heaven."- Hebrews 1:3 (NIV)

GOD is the incomprehensible Creator existing outside of space and time and thus is unknowable and unsearchable. GOD is also immanent; He is present in all of creation, while remaining distinct from it. In other words, there is no place where GOD is not present. His sovereign control extends everywhere simultaneously. In a simple word, He is very much involved with His creation and with His people and the details of our lives.

The Bible says in 2 Kings 4:1, NIV- *"A certain woman of the wives of the sons of the prophets cried out to Elisha, saying, "Your servant my husband is dead, and you know that your servant feared the Lord. And the creditor is coming to take my two sons to be his slaves."* GOD usually meets the needs of His people through people, especially believers ministering to other believers. A widow was appealing to the Lord, she sought help through Prophet Elisha based on these two facts:

As one of the sons of the prophets, her husband had been a servant and student of Prophet Elisha's ministry.

Her husband had been faithful to the Lord.

"Elisha replied to her, "How can I help you? Tell me, what do you have in your house?" "Your servant has nothing there at all," she said, *"except a small jar of olive oil."*- 2 Kings 4:2 (NIV)

As a man of GOD, Prophet Elisha represented the person, power, and care of GOD. Elisha was available to both the destitute and kings. GOD had acted powerfully first in Elijah and then in Elisha to authenticate His covenant care for His people.

When Elisha asked, *"What shall I do for you?,"* he was in essence saying, what do you want GOD to do for you through me?

"You desire but do not have, so you kill. You covet but you cannot get what you want, so you quarrel and fight. You do not have because you do not ask God." – James 4:2 (NIV)

There is no question that one of our great failures is our failure in prayer. Though we are always to ask according to the will of GOD and pure motives, we are still commanded to take our needs to the Lord and to entreat others to pray for us.

> ***"If you remain in me and my words remain in you, ask whatever you wish, and it will be done for you."*** - John 15:7 (NIV)

GOD wants us to come to Him as His children and in faith, with His glory always in view, to ask for our needs according to the perfect will of GOD. Too often we either take GOD for granted or act as though He does not care or He cannot see us.

Interestingly, Prophet Elisha did not wait for widow's answer. Why? Well, because her needs were obvious and she had already come to him and declared her problem which also indicated her request-- income to pay off her financial obligation and save her sons from slavery.

> ***"Do not be like them, for your Father knows what you need before you ask him."*** - Mathew 6:8 (NIV)

GOD knows our needs before we ask; in fact, He has known them from all eternity before we were created. GOD and His son, Jesus Christ knows us fully. He knows our names (Isaiah 43:1), our addresses (Acts 9:11), our strengths and weaknesses (Psalm 27:1), our family history, our DNA and biological makeup (Jeremiah 1:5) and our worldview. He knows every nook and cranny of us. GOD knows us better than we know ourselves (Isaiah 49:6).

GOD knows our sufferings. Jesus Christ, the Son of GOD also knows suffering on an intense, personal level. Jesus' knowledge of suffering is not abstract, ivory tower, textbook knowledge.

"He was despised and rejected by mankind, a man of suffering, and familiar with pain. Like one from whom people hide their faces he was despised, and we held him in low esteem."- Isaiah 53:3 (NIV)

Jesus Christ was a man of sorrows. He was mocked, betrayed, and humiliated for our sakes.

"About three in the afternoon Jesus cried out in a loud voice, "Eli, Eli, lema sabachthani?" (which means *"My God, my God, why have you forsaken me?"*)."- Mathew 27:46 (NIV)

As He hung on the cross He was cut off from His Father. Jesus Christ knew excruciating, overwhelming, and crushing sorrow.

Then why do we need to ask? Because praying to GOD causes us to be dependent on GOD; it demonstrates our faith and demonstrates that it is He who ultimately meets our needs.

"May the LORD, the God of your ancestors, increase you a thousand times and bless you as he has promised!"- Deuteronomy 1:11 (NIV)

The widow was so destitute, that the only thing she had was this oil, which was used for anointing the body or for cooking--or she may have been saving it for her burial. But there is a principle here which we find repeated in Scripture: the way GOD generally meets our needs is to take what we have and to multiply it as we turn our lives over to Him and obey the principles of His Word. This is true of our talents, gifts, finances, or physical assets.

We need to investigate what we have in all areas and then, use those blessings as good stewards of GOD's grace, however small they may seem, surrender them to the Lord and trust the Lord to bless and provide as He sees fit.

But many today want to win the sweepstakes or lottery rather than have to trust GOD with whatever He has allotted them. Sometimes GOD does supply from places unknown and in ways beyond our imagination. But our responsibility is to take what we have no matter how small or large and turn it over to Him to multiply.

"Then go inside and shut the door behind you and your sons. Pour oil into all the jars, and as each is filled, put it to one side."- 2 Kings 4:4 (NIV)

Furthermore, Elisha's absence when the miracle took place would demonstrate that the power came from GOD alone, not Elisha. This was certainly designed to encourage her to greater faith and dependence on the Lord. Devout faith and obedience produces an abundance of spiritual blessings.

The Bible says in Philippians 4:19, NIV —"**And my God shall supply all your need according to His riches in glory by Christ Jesus.**" Whatever needs you have, GOD wants you to know that His supply will be there for you. You have His Word for it today. He promises that He will supply all your needs, not just some. And He will supply all your needs according to His riches. This means that He will speak to everything He has created to work for you and not against you. Depend on GOD alone; put your hope in Him. He alone will provide, protect, defend, and we shall never be defeated in Jesus' name. Amen.

Chapter Sixteen: The Mercy of GOD

"And the LORD commanded the fish, and it vomited Jonah onto dry land" - Jonah 2:10 (NIV)

From Jonah Chapter One, I find Prophet Jonah actions hard to believe. Jonah speaks too much of himself, of his experience, of his danger, of his agony. He speaks too little of GOD, he was acting like a pagan while the pagan sailors feared the Lord and worshiped the GOD of heaven and earth.

"At this the men greatly feared the Lord, and they offered a sacrifice to the Lord and made vows to him"- Jonah 1:16 (NIV)

GOD spared Jonah's life by a means that appeared to be his destruction, a giant fish. Jonah was drowning, he was enveloped in darkness, and around him were slimy walls of flesh. The odor must have been ugly. He had been swallowed by a fish! It was an even slower and horrible death than he had anticipated; only moments of life remained. While inside the fish, Jonah composed a prayer as recorded in Jonah Chapter 2. At the end of the day, what supposed to be his destruction was actually his salvation.

The Bible says in Jonah 4:1, NIV-" ***But to Jonah this seemed very wrong, and he became angry"***. This is absolutely amazing, someone that was wrong and he was protesting. He protested against GOD on the basis of His mercy, compassion, loving-kindness, and turning from calamity. This is the only place in the Bible where a person protested against GOD for being merciful. Jonah was angry about GOD's mercy. He was angry that GOD showed mercy to the Ninevites.

> *"But the LORD said, "You have been concerned about this plant, though you did not tend it or make it grow. It sprang up overnight and died overnight"*- Jonah 4:10 (NIV)

He was happy that GOD showed mercy to him in the shade plant, but he became furious when GOD took it away. Jonah did not deserve that plant, and he most certainly did not earn it. It was a gift of GOD's mercy, and GOD could give it or, just as freely, take it away.

Jonah wanted GOD's blessings. He expected GOD's blessings. And he was angry when GOD took those blessings away. He wanted the benefits and blessings of GOD, but as one who deserved them rather than as an unworthy sinner who did not deserve them. This is what angered Jonah about GOD's dealings with the Ninevites. GOD's grace and mercy humbles the recipient, GOD's indicates the unworthiness of the recipient. Jonah wanted to be blessed, but not on the grounds of grace.

> *"All of us have become like one who is unclean, and all our righteous acts are like filthy rags; we all shrivel up like a leaf, and like the wind our sins sweep us away"*- Isaiah 64:6 (NIV)

Jonah was self-righteous. Self-righteous people do not want to confess their sins and ask GOD for mercy and grace. They think they are worthy of GOD's blessings, and they are only angry when GOD does not jump through their hoops and fulfill all their desires.

The Bible says in Romans 3:23, NIV that **"for all have sinned and fall short of the glory of God"**. Let me ask you, if you have ever been mad at GOD like Jonah. I venture to say that you have, whether you recognize and admit it or not. And why were you mad at GOD? Because you felt GOD did not give you what you deserved. You were mad because GOD was not dealing with you on the basis of something other than grace. Grace is not obliged to give the unworthy sinner anything. And the unworthy sinner has no grounds for protest if GOD withholds His grace, for it was not something he earned or deserved anyway.

"If you had known what these words mean, 'I desire mercy, not sacrifice, you would not have condemned the innocent."- Mathew 12:7 (NIV)

GOD's mercy is the rule of life, and it is also the dominant theme of our lives as we live in this complex world and serve in the Body of Christ. We are to show mercy to others, just as GOD has been merciful to us.

If you would receive the grace of GOD, you must do so by accepting the merciful gift of salvation that GOD has provided in and through His Son, Jesus Christ. May our hearts and minds be continually awe-struck with the Mercy of GOD.

Heaven Is Real

Chapter Seventeen:
Heaven Is Real

"I declare to you, brothers and sisters, that flesh and blood cannot inherit the kingdom of God, nor does the perishable inherit the imperishable."- 1 Corinthians 15:50 (NIV)

Apostle Paul explains that a natural human body consists of flesh and blood as we know, it is unsuitable for Heaven. I was driving through one of the cities in Pennsylvania when I noticed this sign in a store: *""No shoes, no shirt, no service."* This means that one's appearance and attire has to meet certain standards, or he or she is not welcome. That is the way Heaven is. Apostles Paul makes it clear to us that we can't go to Heaven just as we are today. No matter how healthy, strong, and handsome or beautiful we may be, we are unfit for Heaven. We can't have a decaying body in a permanent home. Heaven is a place where there is no pain, no sorrow, no sickness, or death. These perishable bodies that we possess here on earth are not suited for Heaven.

The Bible says in 1 Corinthians 15:51, NIV - *"Listen, I tell you a mystery: We will not all sleep, but we will all be changed"*. When my three children were little, and fell asleep in the living room. I picked them and carried them to their respective bedrooms. When they woke up in the morning they found themselves in another rooms. Then we ask me, *"Dad, how did we get to our rooms"*? Death for the Christian is like that. You go to sleep in one room and wake up in another. In light of this reality, we should not fear death, whether we sleep or take part in the rapture. We should have supreme confidence that we will be with our Lord Jesus Christ. The death and burial of our earthly bodies is not an unfortunate circumstance; it is a necessity in order to go to Heaven, they must be transformed into a glorified body so that we can be, and live in GOD's presence before His perfection, glory, holiness, and beauty.

The Bible says in 1 Corinthians 15:54-55, NIV- **"When the perishable has been clothed with the imperishable, and the mortal with immortality, then the saying that is written will come true: "Death has been swallowed up in victory."** Where, O death, is your sting?." A boy and his father were out for a ride when a bee flew in the car window. The little boy, who was allergic to bee stings, was afraid. The father quickly reached out, grabbed the bee, squeezed it in his hand, and killed the bee that wanted to sting his boy. His father reached out his hand, but this time he pointed to his palm, the bee stung the father while he was trying to kill the bee. **"Do you see this?"** he asked. **"You don't need to be afraid anymore. I have taken the sting for you."** In a similar way, Jesus Christ our Savior came to our rescue and took the sting for us and we no longer have to fear death. Though death may buzz over us and land on us it can do no harm and one day death itself will die (Revelation 20:14, paraphrase)

I love church planting. I led a church planting initiative to the City of Reading in 2009. GOD took me to Heaven after a late evening telephone prayer conference with our new members in this newly formed parish church that GOD used me to plant. As I was about to stand up because I was on my knees throughout the prayer session. I saw my spirit jumped out of my body and the body was on the floor. There is a 'spiritual' hedge around us as Christians. Remember, the story of Job; how Satan argues with GOD:

"Have you not put a hedge around him and his household and everything he has? You have blessed the work of his hands, so that his flocks and herds are spread throughout the land.'"-Job 1:10 (NIV).

We too are hedged all around with GOD's powerful protection as children of faith. Satan can't touch us without His knowledge and GOD has promised not to test us beyond our ability. In a similar way, I was so curious because I trust GOD for His protection even in a difficult assignment. I asked this interesting question without any fear, ***"What happened, and why my spirit was not in the body anymore?"*** There was a response that a spiritual accident has taken place. The first and second angels appeared to me to make sure that there is no iniquity in my life. They didn't see any and they looked very disappointed, shook their heads, and went away. As soon as those two angels completed their assignments, the third Angel that was looking at us from a distant came over to me. The form and appearance of this third angel looked very bright, gloriously, majestically, elegant, and powerful. He said to me that I overcame by the Blood of the Lamb (Revelation 12:11, paraphrase). As soon as this Angel mentioned this statement I found myself at the gate of Heaven. The numerous saints that I have never met while on earth came over to welcome me home. No wonder the Book of Hebrews 12:1-2, NIV says:

"Therefore, since we are surrounded by such a great cloud of witnesses, let us throw off everything that hinders and the sin that so easily entangles. And let us run with perseverance the race marked out for us, fixing our eyes on Jesus, the pioneer and perfecter of faith. For the joy set before him he endured the cross, scorning its shame, and sat down at the right hand of the throne of God."

In other words, the great cloud of witnesses were all those people who have lived before us whether famous or not who have lived lives of faith, followed a true GOD, served Master Jesus, leaving for us a rich spiritual legacy.

The good thing was that these saints in Heaven were radiant with unspeakable joyful. It was as if they have been watching me while I was on earth, they knew me, and they called me by my name. When I looked at their faces I knew their names too, and I remembered everything they did while they were on the earth though I never met them while on earth. They told me that the Master Jesus has prepared a banquet for me. As I was moving from the reception area to the passage where the banquet has been prepared for me where I supposed to meet the Chairman of the banquet, the Lord Jesus Christ. My spirit came back to my body and then woke.

"Nothing in all creation is hidden from God's sight. Everything is uncovered and laid bare before the eyes of him to whom we must give account." - Hebrews 4:13 (NIV)

We cannot hide from GOD; He fills heaven and earth. Time and space are no constraint to Him. He sees your every movement and knows motive behind every decision you take. He sees which shows you are watching and which web sites you are visiting. He hears how you speak to your coworkers, Church members, Pastor and how you gossip about them. He reads your heart and mind. You can't hide.

In Heaven, I remembered that I am the Church Pastor and I remembered our Church congregation and my three children. I thought of the hardship and sorrow they will go through if I am not around. The temperature and joy in Heaven was too much to describe that I wanted to stay there permanently. In Heaven, I prayed to the Lord to take care of my children and congregation. I remembered telling myself that I made it home at last!

The Bible says in 1 Corinthians 15:58, NIV - ***"Therefore, my dear brothers and sisters, stand firm. Let nothing move you. Always give yourselves fully to the work of the Lord, because you know that your labor in the Lord is not in vain."*** Like the Corinthians we are prone to impatient, discouragement, and laziness. We let the circumstances of life blow us out of the water. We allow things we are going through to depress us. Apostle Paul urges us to be ***"always abounding in the work of the Lord."*** No one gets to the Olympics, much less walks away with a medal, who did not give himself or herself fully to their sport. The commitment of those athletes is phenomenal. They give up their comfort zone, privileges, sleep, favorite foods, anything, because of the goal that is before them of winning. So also no one will hear Jesus say, ***"Well done, good and faithful servant,"*** if he does not give himself fully to the work of the Lord.

Let me share another testimony with you. Some years ago, when we used to have two Sunday Services that I had to preach at the two locations (Quakertown, Pennsylvania and Reading, Pennsylvania) which were one hour and twenty minutes apart. One Sunday night, I remember we came back home very late, hungry, tired and very cold. As I laid on the bed too tired to remove my suit clothes and shoes, I was even too tired to eat. I was trying to sleep. GOD's presence and voice filled the room and He said ***"Thank you for taking care of my business"***. At once, I received uncommon strength; it was as if received that I have slept for 8 hours whereas only laid down for less than 15 minutes. I jumped up from the bed, the tiredness and hunger disappeared immediately. This shows that GOD sees and appreciates every effort that we contribute to His Kingdom.

Let me challenge you with this truth, you cannot grow spiritually unless you are serving the Lord and others genuinely. It is absolutely impossible. You might say to me, ***"I attend church, I am reading my Bible, I am praying."*** That is all wonderful! But that does not suggest that you are growing spiritually. Spiritual growth takes place when the Bible changes us and we begin to bless others. The Bible teaches that servant hood makes a man or woman more like our Master, Jesus Christ. Additionally, the Bible promises us great eternal reward for serving Christ in this life.

Chapter Eighteen:
Catching a glimpse of GOD's Glory

"Dear friends, now we are children of God, and what we will be has not yet been made known. But we know that when Christ appears,[a] we shall be like him, for we shall see him as he is." - 1 John 3:2 (NIV).

Many Christians deal with constant friction and tension in their marriages and families. Even though many are devoting more time and energy to marriage and family, many Christians are still unhappy than ever. Consumer world has infiltrated the Church; many people come to Church solely to have their needs and preferences met. When these needs are not met, dissatisfaction occurs. They either leave the Church to go to another or start playing blaming games.

"At once I was in the Spirit, and there before me was a throne in heaven with someone sitting on it."- Revelation 4:2 (NIV).

Looking into Heaven, it was recorded that John the beloved saw GOD the father sitting upon His throne. Can you imagine anything more glorious? Apostle John described the position of a king who is actively reigning. John saw the Lord GOD Almighty actively exercising the duties of His executive office over the affairs of His creation. We all need that experience to transform our reasoning faculty in order to understand the real meaning of life.

> *"I tell you, he will see that they get justice, and quickly. However, when the Son of Man comes, will he find faith on the earth?"*- Luke 18:8 (NIV)

On March 1, 2018, President Putin boasted his military might with animation of Florida nuke strike. The first thing that went to my mind was, GOD where are you? It is easy to ask this question every time we watch the news or read the newspaper. This world is sinking deeper and deeper into a quagmire of sin, while the Christians seem to be busy with their personal agenda but not the agenda of heaven. On February 21, 2018 when Evangelist Billy Graham passed unto glory at age 99, I asked GOD we need more of genuine GOD's generals in this dispensation. It seems the church appears to be making less of an impact upon our culture, some high profile pastors and teachers have fallen into sin. Very few can be trusted because of what we are hearing, or seeing. Pastors and ministers of gospel are busy fighting one another on less important matters while the devil and hosts of hell are busy performing their enterprise.

> *"You are the salt of the earth. But if the salt loses its saltiness, how can it be made salty again? It is no longer good for anything, except to be thrown out and trampled underfoot."*- Mathew 5:13 (NIV)

Some churches have stopped preaching the Gospel altogether. Certain churches have stopped mentioning Holy Ghost or Holy Spirit in their services saying that the word is scary; they put the Spirit of GOD in the back burner. Like salt that has lost its savor, the Church seems to be impotent.

> *"I have told you these things, so that in me you may have peace. In this world you will have trouble. But take heart! I have overcome the world."* -John 16:33 (NIV)

Due to what is going on around the world, it's easy to ask, **"GOD, are you still in control?"** When I was in the Presence of GOD praying one morning, I asked GOD to show me a unique and specific sign that He is hearing me and still in control; within 30minutes He showed me a pronounced sign.

"And, "If it is hard for the righteous to be saved, what will become of the ungodly and the sinner?" - 1 Peter 4:18 (NIV)

As we see the world falling apart all around us we must all be reminded that GOD is doing something. He has not resigned. He has not been impeached, nor put out of office. He is not even up for reelection. There are no term limits to His being GOD.

The Bible says in Matthew 6:26, NIV –**"Look at the birds of the air: they neither sow nor reap nor gather into barns, and yet your heavenly Father feeds them. Are you not of more value than they?"**

Have you looked up lately to see GOD still upon His throne? Have you come to understand that His sovereign throne controls the events of your life? No matter what may seem out of control in your life today, I want you to know that GOD is still in control. Though evil reigns for a time on earth, GOD will ultimately prevail. There is no attribute more comforting to us as GOD's children than His sovereignty. Whatever your trial, whatever your test, whatever you are going through at this point of your life. I want you to know that my GOD and your Creator is still on His throne, sometimes this is the only thing that will keep you and I going.

"And the one who sat there had the appearance of jasper and ruby. A rainbow that shone like an emerald encircled the throne. Surrounding the throne were twenty-four other thrones, and seated on them were twenty-four elders. They were dressed in white and had crowns of gold on their heads."- Revelation 4:3-4 (NIV)

The sovereign Lord GOD Almighty was described in terms of two precious stones, the jasper and the sardius. These stones are used to portray something of GOD's eternal glory, awesome holiness, and majesty. Jasper was a clear, crystal-like gem and a translucent rock. This portrays the purity and brilliance of GOD's holiness.

A sardius stone was blood red, undoubtedly portraying GOD's wrath and justice, but it would also look at His redemptive work of love and grace in the person of the Lamb of GOD who came to take away the sin of the world through His death on the cross.

John the Beloved also saw a rainbow, the rainbow represented GOD's faithfulness to never destroy the world again as He did with the flood. It was also a sign of GOD's mercy, grace, and long suffering. It also means that GOD's grace will endure forever. In the midst of wrath and problems of life, GOD remembers mercy to save and deliver. His mercy and grace are greater than His judgment.

The Bible says in Psalm 8: 3-4, NIV –"**When I consider your heavens, the work of your fingers, the moon and the stars, which you have set in place, what is mankind that you are mindful of them, human beings that you care for them?"**

Astronomers estimated that there are 100 billion stars in our own galaxy and that there may be 100 billion galaxies in the universe. GOD created the human brain that weighs less than three pounds which is the size of a grapefruit, and is thousands of times more powerful than the world's most powerful computer. Your fingerprints are unlike anyone else's fingerprints. The FBI has collected more than 200 million fingerprints and has never found two that are alike.

My GOD and your Father is worthy of praise and worship through His power all things are created and through His purpose and perfect Will He brought you and I and everything into existence and gives meaning to it all. If we refuse to acknowledge the power and purpose of GOD there is judgment waiting for unrepentant and disobedience individuals.

In Revelation 4:4 (paraphrase), the elders have crowns of gold on their heads. These crowns indicate achievement and victory. Faithful believers are also promised five crowns for spiritual accomplishments.

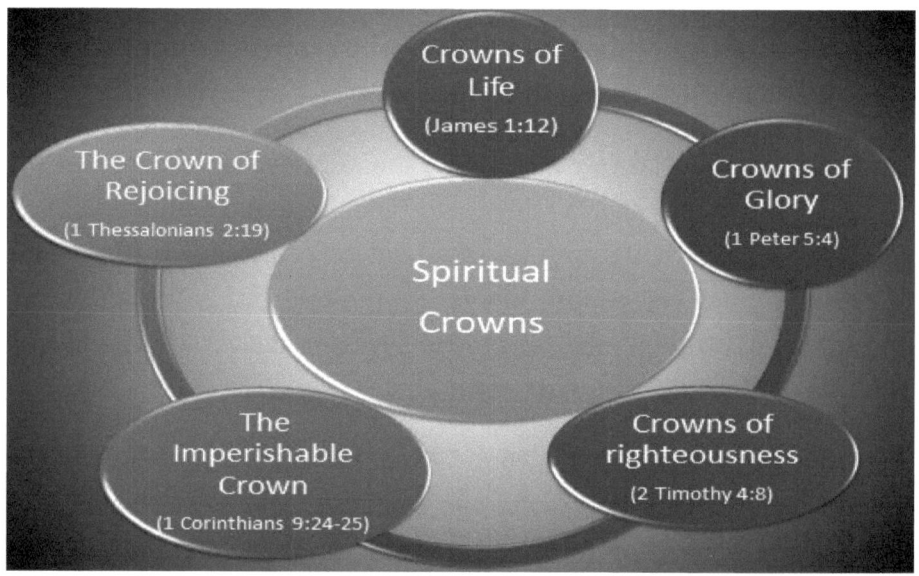

Crowns for spiritual accomplishments

As the elders were seen singing a song of redemption. Someday, we shall join the elders to sing and worship our Heavenly Father in the courtyard of Heaven. My friend, will you be there? Time might not be on your side. Our days are numbered. Times and seasons belong to the Lord. Do not delay any longer, please surrender your life fully by genuinely accept Jesus Christ the Son of GOD as the Lord of your life and start obeying Him.

Chapter Nineteen: Who Will Be in Heaven and What is Heaven Like?

"And I saw a new heaven and a new earth: for the first heaven and the first earth were passed away; and there was no more sea." - Revelation 21: 1 (NKJV)

I have read the Book of Revelation a number of times. I have talked through this Book of Revelation, in our church within the last few years we have studied the Book of Revelation twice from beginning to the end during our weekly Bible Study. But each time I read through the Book of Revelation, my eyeballs roll and adjust my sitting position. I wish I could tell that I have nice, clear picture. I think maybe one of the reasons that the Book of Revelation is written that way is that we ought to get the big picture.

I will like to provoke your critical thinking by just asking a few questions. Who will be in Heaven? What is Heaven like? What will the saints be doing in eternity?

The Bible says in 1 John 3:2, NIV *—"Dear friends, now we are children of God, and what we will be has not yet been made known. But we know that when Christ appears, we shall be like him, for we shall see him as* *he is."*. Obviously, GOD will be there. Father, Son and Holy Spirit will be present in Heaven.

> *"And I will take away mine hand, and thou shalt see my back parts: but my face shall not be seen."* – Exodus 33:23

Moses got a pretty good view of GOD from the back side, but he did not see everything. By GOD's grace and mercy, what we are going to see when we get to Heaven is—we are going to see GOD face to face in all His glory. So, you have GOD the Father, who is described as being there, GOD the Son, who is our Lord Jesus Christ, and then the Holy Spirit.

> *"But I said, "I have labored in vain; I have spent my strength for nothing at all. Yet what is due me is in the Lord's hand, and my reward is with my God."* - Isaiah 49: 4 (NIV)

Shortly before I wrote this passage, it was around 3:00am, I was reading and mediating from the Book of Isaiah and the Lord spoke to me that my labor is not in vain and He will not forget me.

Likewise, in Heaven there are the saints, and I think there is a special honor that is given to those who have labored genuinely in the Kingdom of GOD; some are the martyrs, who have died for their faith in the Lord Jesus, many of them in the great tribulation.

> *"But you have come to Mount Zion, to the city of the living God, the heavenly Jerusalem. You have come to thousands upon thousands of angels in joyful assembly"* – Hebrews 12:22 (NIV)

In Heaven there are angels. Lots of angels are there and I think we would probably expect that. There will be billions of angels' ministering to GOD in His court in Heaven.

> *"Also in front of the throne there was what looked like a sea of glass, clear as crystal. In the center, around the throne, were four living*

creatures, and they were covered with eyes, in front and in back."-
Revelation 4:6 (NIV)

Does that not just bend your mind? I think there is a tendency, at least in my mind, to think of Heaven in terms of me and all my fellow human beings that are saved and then the angels, and pretty much GOD, Jesus Christ and Holy Spirit and that is it. In addition, there will be four living creatures that are obviously beyond our dimension.

"Surrounding the throne were twenty-four other thrones, and seated on them were twenty-four elders. They were dressed in white and had crowns of gold on their heads."- Revelation 4: 4 (NIV)

There are twenty four elders in Heaven. They occur about 12 times in the Book of Revelation. The Book of Revelation nowhere specifically identifies who the twenty-four elders are.

"if we endure, we will also reign with him. If we disown him, he will also disown us" - 2 Timothy 2:12 (NIV)

However, they are most likely representative of the Church. It is unlikely that they are angelic beings. The fact that they sit on thrones indicates that they reign with our Lord Jesus Christ. Nowhere in Scripture do angels ever rule or sit on thrones. Another thought is that the golden crowns worn by the twenty elders also indicate these are men, not angels. Crowns are never promised to angels, nor are angels ever seen wearing them. The word translated *"crown"* refers to the victor's crown, worn by those who have successfully competed and won the victory as Jesus Christ promised us in Book of James 1:12, NIV:

"Blessed is the man who remains steadfast under trial, for when he has stood the test he will receive the crown of life, which God has promised to those who love him."

We are not the only people who will be in Heaven, but we are the only bride. The beauty of it is that when we are gathered together and assembled before GOD Almighty, we are going to be His bride and the object of His great affection and love.

The Bible says in Isaiah 6:3, NIV – *"And they were calling to one another: 'Holy, holy, holy is the Lord Almighty; the whole earth is full of his glory.'"*

What is heaven like? Heaven is like GOD. Have you ever gone to somebody's house and looked at their house and you say that is just you. In my house, I have paintings; I love those paintings to provoke my thinking, some of them are pretty good view. Sometimes we say that about the way people dress. Somehow that is just them. When we get to Heaven, it is going to be just GOD. It is so GOD-like, I think, in these ways. Think about glory. Heaven will be glorious.

"The city does not need the sun or the moon to shine on it, for the glory of God gives it light, and the Lamb is its lamp." – Revelation 21:23 (NIV)

So, here the glory of GOD is such a bright radiance you do not need any other light. It is a glorious place.

"Nothing impure will ever enter it, nor will anyone who does what is shameful or deceitful, but only those whose names are written in the Lamb's book of life."- Revelation 21:27 (NIV)

Heaven is a holy place.

"I declare to you, brothers and sisters, that flesh and blood cannot inherit the kingdom of God, nor does the perishable inherit the imperishable." – 1 Corinthians 15:50 (NIV)

No mortal can see immortal GOD; death should not make us to be upset and afraid. For us to die as believers is a big gain. When we leave this body, we will be transformed into a new body in order to be able to come into the presence of GOD.

What is Heaven Like? Heaven is the prototype of Jesus Christ. In Matthew 1:23, Jesus Christ was called Emanuel, **"GOD with us."** Likewise in John 1:14 (paraphrase), ***"He tabernacle amongst us."*** So, there are those indications that our Lord Jesus is certainly GOD dwelling amongst men and that, of course, is what Heaven is about.

"Jesus answered: "Don't you know me, Philip, even after I have been among you such a long time? Anyone who has seen me has seen the Father. How can you say, 'Show us the Father'?" - John 14:9 (NIV)

We see that in our Lord Jesus Christ the attributes of GOD are all displayed through the humanity of our Lord Jesus, He certainly converted things that of lesser value into greater value.

And the last one is joy. Heaven is going to be a joyous place because it is a reflection of GOD. There will be great reunion, all our Christian loved ones and relatives that we didn't have the opportunity to meet on this earth we shall meet them in Heaven. There will be celebration till eternity.

So, what are we going to be doing in Heaven? We will be singing. We will be singing a new song. GOD gave me a snapshot of what we will be doing in Heaven. It was on a Friday around 6:00pm in the year 2015. I was at a corporate office clearing my desk to get ready for the weekend. When I looked at the right side of a wall in my office, GOD opened my eyes to see a glimpse of Heaven in about 30secs, it was a big celebration, and people were dancing, jumping, rolling up as high to about 20 feet high and singing in different languages and playing drums. We are going to be perfect and we will not have as much trouble anymore.

My focus prayer points for you are that GOD should give you an appetite for Heaven and that He should help you to look forward to that day when we will not only be in Heaven, but we will be just like HIM. GOD shall keep us to the end in Jesus' name. Amen.

Finishing Strong

Chapter Twenty:
Your Toiling and Pains Shall Be Over

"And Simon answered and said, Master, we toiled all night, and took nothing: but at thy word I will let down the nets." - Luke 5:5 (NIV)

I must confess that I am reading somewhat between the lines, but I suspect that the disciples were fearful concerning the very practical matter of providing for themselves and their families. The longer these men were with Jesus, the more they wanted to be with Him all the time. But you see, they had responsibilities and financial obligations to consider, too. I can just see Peter, telling his wife that he would love to be able to go with Jesus Christ when He traveled to more distant places. His wife might be protesting, But Peter, **"How can we pay the bills?"** The children need clothes, the roof on the house needs repair, and you know that we have to care for my mother ..."

"When he had finished speaking, he said to Simon, "Put out into deep water, and let down the nets for a catch.""- Luke 5:4 (NIV)

Peter and other disciples decided to go fishing in order to meet their physical and material needs. On the sea, they had worked hard all night to catch the fish. Peter indicates that their efforts had been futile. Night was the best time to fish. If they had not caught anything at night, why in the world should they catch anything in the daytime, the worst possible time to fish?

"When they had done so, they caught such a large number of fish that their nets began to break."- Luke 5:6 (NIV)

This miracle with the fish demonstrated in a very remarkable way that Jesus Christ is not only to be trusted as Teacher and Prophet and Miracle-worker, but also as their great Provider. With this remarkable catch, Jesus shows that He is able to provide. He is sovereign in the matter of work, as well as in all other matters.

"Ah, Sovereign Lord, you have made the heavens and the earth by your great power and outstretched arm. Nothing is too hard for you."
- Jeremiah 32:17 (NIV)

Jesus Christ is always looking for opportunity to take toiling out of our lives, and get us back to the priority of our assignment rather than just working for a living. As we can see from this story, Jesus Christ didn't just meet disciples' needs; He abundantly supplied all that they wanted.

The Bible says in John 21:6, NIV -" He said, *"Throw your net on the right side of the boat and you will find some."* When they did, they were unable to haul the net in because of the large number of fish."

We need, however to understand this truth that GOD never abandon us. Disciples at the point of their lives might be thinking that their Master, Jesus Christ has abandoned them, especially after His death, until He miraculously delivers them from toiling. Think about this for a moment. Jesus Christ could have risen, and go back to heaven to enjoy His glory in heaven. Many people, in fact, believe this is exactly what Jesus Christ could have done after intense suffering and agony on the cross. But this is not true. Jesus Christ didn't put the disciples on this journey and abandoned them to figure things out themselves.

I want you to know as well that you aren't where you are by accident or by happenstance; you are there because GOD permitted it. Long before the world was created, GOD knew all about you, and He had planned to make a way of escape for you. Before eternity began, you were part of His agenda. For instance, you didn't have any chance about whether you will be born or not. GOD had chosen to give you life.

> *"Before I formed you in the womb I knew[a] you, before you were born I set you apart; I appointed you as a prophet to the nations."*-
> Jeremiah 1:5 (NIV)

In another word, the mechanics at the dealership likely will be very familiar with the make and model of your car than general auto repair shops. Likewise, we originated from GOD, and our greatest joy will be derived by giving ourselves back to Him, and then learn to walk with Him daily until He calls us back home. One of the main reasons I called GOD my daddy is that when the situation is challenging, many times, I have seen His Mighty Hands in my situations.

> *"The Lord himself goes before you and will be with you; he will never leave you nor forsake you. Do not be afraid; do not be discouraged."*-
> Deuteronomy 31:8 (NIV)

GOD didn't only have a plan for you. He is ready to be with you, only if you will allow Him. You don't need to be alone, He wants to be with you and help you. GOD cares for you, and want to help you.

> *"When you pass through the waters, I will be with you; And through the rivers, they shall not overflow you. When you walk through the fire, you shall not be burned, Nor shall the flame scorch you."*-Isaiah
> 43:2 (NKJV)

No matter what happens, GOD will never abandon you because He made you in His own in image, you are for Him and you belong to Him. He understands you more than anybody. He knows your composition. He sees beyond ordinary- He knows the reasons behind your situation. Though, it might not be possible to change the past, but with GOD's help you can change the future. But He doesn't want you to be shackled by the past. He wants to free you from toiling and put your feet on a brand new future and hope in Jesus Christ.

Let that walk with Him begins today.

The Bible says in Psalm 8:5, NIV -" ***For You have made him a little lower than the angels, And You have crowned him with glory and honor.***" We are uniquely created. GOD created us to have a personal relationship with Him. In another word, He created us to be His friends. This was the original divine plan right from the beginning when Adam and Eve were created in the Garden of Eden.

"And they heard the [a]sound of the Lord God walking in the garden in the cool of the day, and Adam and his wife hid themselves from the presence of the Lord God among the trees of the garden." - Genesis 3:8 (NKJV)

Our friendship with GOD is with a difference. On a human level, we chose friends who share similar interests or kindred personalities. But GOD and humans are not equals. GOD is the Sovereign Ruler of the universe, the all-powerful Creator; He made everything, and controls and sustains it by His power. GOD is also everywhere at the same time. He is also the all-knowing GOD who sees everything that happens.

" And there is no creature hidden from His sight, but all things are naked and open to the eyes of Him to whom we must give account." - Hebrews 4:13 (NKJV)

GOD is unlimited, humans are limited. GOD is independent. Humans are dependent- people depend on ecological systems for clean water to drink, good soil for food, and for clean air to breath. These are the things GOD created. He didn't create us because He was lonely or because He needed someone to love Him in return. GOD is complete in Himself. He lacks nothing. GOD is self-existent. This means that He had no creator, but always exists, and unchanging.

In spite of the vast difference between GOD and humans, GOD still wants to be humans' friends. This was why we are created. GOD's plan for Adam and Eve is also true for us. GOD has not changed and neither has His purpose.

> *"For what profit is it to a man if he gains the whole world, and loses his own soul? Or what will a man give in exchange for his soul?"* - Matthew 16:26 (NIV)

Jesus Christ stated that our souls are more valuable than all the rest of the world put together. Our body will cease to live someday, but our souls will never die. Your soul is so valuable that GOD sent His Son, Jesus Christ to die and to redeem that soul from eternal destruction in hell.

> *" So God created man in His own image; in the image of God He created him; male and female He created them."* - Genesis 1:27 (NKJV)

GOD gave us a unique spiritual nature. He created us in His own image. The real you is your soul. Your body is a case that's housing your soul. You are very important to GOD because He implanted part of Himself within you. Your soul set you apart from every other living creature, that makes us unique and that makes us fully human.

> *" I say to you that likewise there will be more joy in heaven over one sinner who repents than over ninety-nine [a]just persons who need no repentance."* - Luke 15:7 (NKJV)

One saved soul makes all Heaven rejoice, but GOD is hurting when a soul goes to eternal damnation in hell. If the Angels of Heaven rejoice over every soul that's saved, let them rejoice because of you today, ask GOD to forgive your sins, enter into relationship with Jesus Christ by confessing Him as your Lord and Savior. He will write your name in the Book of life. He will replace your toiling and unnecessary anxiety with

His blissful peace. He will give you a new family and new relationship with Himself and makes you a citizen of His Kingdom in Heaven.

Chapter Twenty-One: No Fear No Fall

I have good news for someone; the protection of GOD shall be evident upon you and your family. You will not fall, so don't be afraid.

"But He said, "You cannot see My face; for no man shall see Me, and live." 21 And the Lord said, "Here is a place by Me, and you shall stand on the rock. 22 So it shall be, while My glory passes by, that I will put you in the cleft of the rock, and will cover you with My hand while I pass by."- Exodus 33:20-22 (NKJV)

GOD spoke to Moses "face to face," but He would not allow Moses to "see His face." Therefore, seeing GOD "face to face" is not the same thing as seeing GOD's face. Speaking "face to face" means speaking with someone on a personal, intimate basis as a friend speaks to a friend. GOD's presence is with His people, and He made that presence known. But nowhere did anyone see the face of GOD, because GOD has no face. GOD is Spirit and is not made of flesh. He is invisible to men because He has no body, and He becomes visible to men by various means. GOD is invisible. GOD cannot be fully seen. Yet, His protection to those that belong to Him is evident.

"You shall not be afraid of the terror by night, Nor of the arrow that flies by day, Nor of the pestilence that walks in darkness, Nor of the destruction that lays waste at noonday." – Psalm 91:5-6 (NKJV)

The source of our safety is GOD Almighty, no threat or danger, no matter how great, is mightier than GOD's keeping power. GOD gives us 24-hour protection. There is no threat, whether seen or unseen, anticipated or unexpected, which can catch GOD unaware and unable to protect us. Though, people are very interested in statistics but statistics don't impress GOD, nor do they impede His protection. No matter how disproportionate the odds, GOD's protection is certain. GOD is able to keep us from all dangers.

"And the Lord will make a difference between the livestock of Israel and the livestock of Egypt. So nothing shall die of all that belongs to the children of Israel."' " Then the Lord appointed a set time, saying, "Tomorrow the Lord will do this thing in the land." So the Lord did this thing on the next day, and all the livestock of Egypt died; but of the livestock of the children of Israel, not one died." – Exodus 9:4-6 (NKJV)

Not only are we safe from the opposition of wicked men and the forces of evil, we are also protected from the righteous wrath of GOD. The plagues in Exodus Chapter 9 were the judgment of GOD, the Egyptians may not have chosen to believe it, but GOD was clearly judging the gods of Egypt and those who would worship them. When GOD's judgment comes upon men, He will let them know what is happening and why. When GOD is disciplining one of His saints, He will be sure to let that saint know what is going on. We need not agonize, searching for hidden sin, at the onslaught of every adversity and affliction. When GOD chastens us for sin, we will know about it.

When GOD is punishing men for sin, He is not silent about it. When He is silent at the time of the suffering of a saint, this is a test of our faith, not an evidence of GOD's judgment. Even Christians sometimes minimize the sin in their lives, and when they do so they fail to take sin seriously. Sin is serious business.

> ***"For the Scripture says to the Pharaoh, "For this very purpose I have raised you up, that I may show My power in you, and that My name may be declared in all the earth."*** *– Romans 9: 17 (NKJV)*

GOD raised Pharaoh up for the purpose of hardening his heart and thus providing the occasion for GOD to manifest His power to men. GOD raised up Pharaoh and hardened Pharaoh's heart in order to promote His own glory. Sometimes GOD will glorify Himself through showing mercy; sometimes GOD will glorify Himself through a man's hardness. GOD wants to demonstrate His Power in our lives through His mighty Hands of Protection. GOD's protection can conquer any odds or probabilities.

Having GOD as a shelter and refuge gives strength and courage to the people of GOD - when GOD's people are stuck deep in fear, it is an indication that they fall short of proper trust in GOD as protector and comforter. The protection of those who abide under the shadow of the Almighty should wipe away all unwarranted fear. Not to be afraid is in itself an unspeakable blessing, with GOD as our shield; we need not dread the opposition of either human or superhuman forces. With GOD as our refuge we should not fear and we cannot fall. We will certainly not fall under GOD's wrath and neither will we fall under the terror of any other.

The Bible says in Psalm 91:11-13, NIV –"***For he will command his angels concerning you to guard you in all your ways; they will lift you up in their hands, so that you will not strike your foot against a stone. You will tread on the lion and the cobra; you will trample the great lion and the serpent***".

GOD's protection was intended to put away unhealthy fears and to prevent us from falling, therefore, no fear and no fall. Fear is a paralyzing force. It causes us to become passive, rather than to be aggressive. Fear keeps us from taking initiative and doing anything which is not "safe." Once our inhibiting fears are swept aside by an appreciation of our safety in GOD's care, we need not be reticent and retiring. We can boldly confront and even defeat the most fearful opponent. We will take on "lions and cobras" because we know we are safe in GOD's keeping, even in the midst of danger.

> *"With long life I will satisfy him and show him my salvation"*- Psalm 91:16 (NIV)

GOD's promise is that we should not fear for we cannot fall and He cannot fail. More than just to help us, GOD has promised to honor us. GOD says of the one who knows His name (Psalm 91:14, paraphrase). This means that GOD will do far more than merely **"save us by the skin of our teeth"**. He will deliver us with dignity and glory. GOD's deliverance one step further - GOD will not only save us from death, He will give us long life. Today, I believe this promise is for the children of GOD who are in the right standing with GOD. In another word, the promise of GOD's help is for those who are personally related to Him.

The Bible says in Psalm 91:15, NIV —"He will call on me, and I will answer him; I will be with him in trouble, I will deliver him and honor him." Finally, those whom GOD protects are those who petition Him to do so. Those who recognize their peril and ask for GOD's protection, receive it. Everyone's most urgent need is deliverance from the ultimate danger. If you have never come to a personal faith in GOD, you must first recognize your sinful condition and the danger which this creates. You are a sinner, condemned by GOD's righteous law, and destined to eternal punishment. Jesus Christ offers you the forgiveness of your sins and the safety of eternal life in the presence of GOD by acknowledging your sin and trusting in Christ's death in your place.

There is danger in not taking GOD's judgement and protection seriously enough. By calling upon Him for salvation, you will be delivered from the danger of divine wrath and given the free gift of eternal life in the presence of GOD.

Chapter Twenty-Two:
What You Started, You Must Finish It

"Thus the heavens and the earth, and all the host of them, were finished." - Genesis 2:1 (NKJV)

We can see from this verse that GOD is not only a starter, but He doesn't stop there, He finishes what He starts! For us to conform to the image of our Heavenly Father we must not be a master of starting things, we must finish what we start, whether it is in ministry assignment, marriage or career. Starting a task, but not finishing, does not give glory to GOD. Starting a task, but not understanding the big picture, and finishing wrong does not help anyone. We have to make up our mind to be finishers in spite of obstacles, not because it is exciting or fun, but because that's what GOD does, and we want to conform to His image. GOD is a finisher, Jesus is a finisher. We must be a finisher too.

The Bible says in Philippians 1:6, NIV - **"Being confident of this, that he who began a good work in you will carry it on to completion until the day of Christ Jesus"**. I want you to know that what matters is not how you start out, but how you finish. Every character in the Bible other than Daniel, Abel and Enoch, had something negative in their lives. They were not perfect initially, yet GOD called them men and women of faith. Be encouraged that GOD uses imperfect people, and be reminded that GOD does not give up on us even though we make mistakes in life. When we think we have failed too many times, He stands ready to achieve His best through us because GOD is merciful (Exodus 34:6)

"I have fought the good fight, I have finished the race, I have kept the faith" - 2 Timothy 4:7 (NIV)

Let us look at Jacob the son of Isaac and Rebecca, the one who finished strong. Jacob started off a little shaky in his life. He deceived his brother under his mother's direction, but against his better judgment.

He was forced to flee his home to avoid his brother's wrath. But once again, GOD brought good out of a bad situation. By leaving his home and going to his mother's relatives, he met his wives, and most importantly, he met GOD. Jacob's life should encourage us as to see GOD's hand in every step of the way. He started out as a deceiving, self-centered young man. But once he came face to face with GOD, his life was never the same again. Even his name had to be changed because of his life change. GOD took an imperfect man, changed him, and used him to fulfill His promise to Abraham. And at the end of his life, he was worshiping GOD. That's how it should be.

The Bible says in Psalm 27:14, NIV-" **Wait for the Lord; be strong and take heart and wait for the Lord."**. Sometimes GOD has to cripple us before we let go of our self-sufficiency and depend on His all-sufficiency. In every situation, GOD wants us to depend and wait on Him. Waiting on GOD is not easy, but the end result is worth it. Trust that He is in control and His timing is perfect. Take some time to be honest with GOD. Tell Him how you are feeling about what is going on around you today. Then leave it in His loving hands. I want you to know those disappointments, emptiness, self-pity, anger, strife, doubt, fear and hopelessness before you right now will be replaced with His Peace If you hold onto Him. If you are not holding onto GOD, what are you holding onto? You cannot finish strong without holding on to GOD because our strength has limit and GOD's is limitless.

Behind every great men and women are interesting stories. A close look at the life of David revealed that GOD plans sometimes work in mysterious ways. There is nothing that GOD cannot do in our lives if we are willing to hold on to GOD steadfastly. All the pain and struggles we face are simply the elements GOD uses to mold us into greatness.

"The Lord is my strength and my shield; my heart trusts in him, and he helps me. My heart leaps for joy, and with my song I praise him." - Psalm 28:7 (NIV)

David was anointed by GOD to be King; David first had to fight against those who were trying to kill him. For years he was forced to wander throughout the desert and seek shelter in caves. That time of struggle brought David to the understanding that his future was ordained by GOD and no one could stop him from accomplishing what he has started. In the midst of David's troubles was a faithful GOD providing all that he needed for victory and to fulfill his plans in David's life. The same is true for you today, GOD has not forgotten you. He knows what you are going through. Don't give up; GOD will finish what He started. Those trials are set for a time and soon your tears will turn to joy in Jesus' name. Amen.

Chapter Twenty-Three:
Finishing Well and Finishing Strong

A man was trying hypnosis to help him lose his weight. His friend asked whether he thought it would work. "Sure," he said, "it worked the last time I tried it!" Let's face it: starting well is relatively easy. Finishing well is a different matter! Starting that new diet or exercise program is kind of fun, but hanging in over the long haul is the real test. Getting married is exciting and relatively easy. Staying married through the struggles, adjustments, and trials is not always an easy matter.

The same is true of the Christian life, same true of being a Father. Becoming a dad is relatively easy, but then comes the hard part—hanging in there as a Christian Father in a world that is hostile towards GOD and His people. The world constantly dangles in front of you all that it has to offer in opposition to the things of GOD.

The Christian life is a marathon, not a 100-yard dash. Since finishing a marathon well is not easy, when you see a man who sprints across the finish line, you ought to try to find out his secret. Apostle Peter was such a man. It's as if he has crossed the finish line with energy to spare.

The Bible says in 1 Peter 5:10, NIV –"***And the God of all grace, who called you to his eternal glory in Christ, after you have suffered a little while, will himself restore you and make you strong, firm and steadfast***".

Apostle Peter is a changed man from the Peter of the Gospels (John 13:8-9). And his teaching is vastly different from what we would have expected of him from the Gospel accounts. His teaching is also very different from much that is taught in Christian circles.

"To the elders among you, I appeal as a fellow elder and a witness of Christ's sufferings who also will share in the glory to be revealed: Be shepherds of God's flock that is under your care, watching over them—not because you must, but because you are willing, as God wants you to be; not pursuing dishonest gain, but eager to serve" – 1 Peter 5:1-2(NIV)

The fathers are the elders. The elders are not necessarily appointed democratically nor do they rule democratically. Ultimately, elders are divinely appointed.

"Take heed therefore unto yourselves, and to all the flock, over the which the Holy Ghost hath made you overseers, to feed the church of God, which he hath purchased with his own blood" – Acts 20:28

The elders get the blame when things seem to go wrong. Apostle Peter therefore clarifies how elders or fathers should exercise authority by contrasting the fleshly temptations leaders face with the spiritual characteristics of leadership which were evident in our Lord and which should be exemplified by elders and all others who exercise authority.

"Now it is required that those who have been given a trust must prove faithful." – 1 Corinthians 4:2 (NIV)

Our eternal rewards are not based upon the gifts or office GOD has given us in this life but in our faithfulness in carrying out whatever task He has given each of us.

Evil shepherds or evil elders seek to further their own interests and use the sheep to bring about selfish gain. They look for their rewards now and think of them in temporal and material terms. Those who would shepherd the flock of GOD whether at home or in the Body of Christ must do so with the same mindset every Christian is called to embrace as exemplified in 1 Peter 5:4, NIV:

"And when the Chief Shepherd appears, you will receive the crown of glory that will never fade away."

The Bible says in 1 Peter 5: 5, NIV – *"In the same way, you who are younger, submit yourselves to your elders. All of you, clothe yourselves with humility toward one another, because, "God opposes the proud but shows favor to the humble".*

I have learned that the key to unity and harmony in the family, the key to godly leadership and submissive obedience, is humility. Apostle Peter calls for humility toward GOD and toward each member of the family.

In humility, fathers should exercise their GOD-given authority and self-sacrifice, laying down their lives for the family. In humility, children should follow the leadership of their Godly father. All the member of the family should submit themselves to GOD in humble dependence, looking to Him for their eternal reward at the proper time. Each should cast their cares upon Him who is the Great Shepherd. The elders should cast their shepherding cares on Him, knowing their task is impossible in merely human strength. The younger men should cast their cares upon GOD, looking to Him for their strength and reward as they submit to their leaders.

"Cast all your anxiety on him because he cares for you." – 1 Peter 5:7 (NIV)

As Fathers or elders we should cast our cares upon Him because we know He cares for us. He cares more for us than we care about ourselves. What we worry and fret about is what we feel to be most important. What we worry and fret about is what we don't wish to commit to Him because we trust ourselves more than we trust GOD. In times of suffering, persecution, and affliction, what greater assurance and comfort is there than knowing not only that GOD is good and He is sovereign (in control), but that He cares for us.

The Bible says in 2 Timothy 4: 7, NIV- ***"I have fought the good fight, I have finished the race, I have kept the faith."***

Departing this world will be easier when you know that you are leaving behind a number of people who can carry on with Christ because of your influence. Each of us needs to ask ourselves, "Am I working on that task?"

You can begin at home. Every Christian parent ought to be waging an all-out campaign to train up his or her children to know Christ and walk with Him. It doesn't happen by accident. It begins by setting the example: you must walk in reality with Jesus Christ if you want to impart that to your kids. Beyond that, dads, are you taking the time to read the Bible and pray with your family? Are you making sure that your family gathers with the Lord's people on the Lord's Day for worship and teaching? Do you talk openly at home about spiritual things? Do you apply GOD's Word when there are tensions or trials on the home front?

Beyond your immediate family, you ought to have a vision for reproducing yourself in the lives of others. As a matter of fact, you can only grow in grace through a personal relationship with the Lord Jesus Christ, who teaches you truth from His Word, which you then take out into the rough-and-tumble of real life in the real world. As a father I always tell my children that the ***"curriculum of life"*** cannot be planned or anticipated. With the sovereignty of a loving GOD, the pathway we will tread in this fallen world will be as unique as each one of us.

Keep in focus view of the present so that you can reproduce yourself in others to carry the torch after you. View your life as a sacrifice to GOD. Let the past be past- stop dwelling on the past. You will be able to look back and say that you engaged in the struggle for the sake of Jesus Christ. You didn't drop out of the race. Keep in focus view of the future. Live in view of that day when you will stand before the Lord, the righteous Judge, vindicated by His grace. May the Lord grant us the grace to finish well and strong in Jesus' Name. Amen.

Chapter Twenty-Four: Protect Your Destiny

"A voice says, "Cry out." And I said, "What shall I cry?" "All people are like grass, and all their faithfulness is like the flowers of the field. The grass withers and the flowers fall, because the breath of the Lord blows on them. Surely the people are grass." - Isaiah 40:6-7 (NIV)

I was born on September 9, 1970. I can remember vividly some of the events that happened in 1976 when I was in elementary school at Ibadan, West Africa. Those events look like yesterday. Our lives are here one moment and gone the next.

Our lifespan is compared with grass and breath. While most of us will intellectually acknowledge the fleeting nature of life, but most people are more excited about things that will not matter in eternity.

Someone once said:

"It ought to be the business of every day to prepare for our last day." - Matthew Henry (1662-1714)

"There are two days on my calendar—'Today' and 'That Day.'" - Martin Luther (1483-1546)

Honestly, a day is coming when all that will really matter is how you and I lived our lives for the sake of eternity.

"And Jacob called unto his sons, and said, Gather yourselves together, that I may tell you that which shall befall you in the last days. Gather yourselves together, and hear, ye sons of Jacob; and hearken unto Israel your father."- Genesis 49:1-2

The above passage provides a sobering wakeup call to contemplate both our present and future life. All the twelve of Jacob's sons regardless of their faithfulness have a future with GOD and are blessed by their father, Jacob.

The word expression *"in the last days"* refers to the distant future, including the end of the age and millennium. Jacob's words are doubly important- in many respects, it can be seen as a picture of that very day when we will leave this earth and stand before our Master, the Lord Jesus Christ. All the great men like Abraham, Prophet Elisha, Apostles Paul, Martin Luther, Matthew Henry and so on were once walking on the face of the earth, but they are no more.

The exhortation to give attention to Jacob's words lays emphasis on the importance of what he is about to say. His words are important. In many respects, this can be seen as a picture of that Day when the believer stands before Jesus Christ. So let me ask you *"Are you living for that Day to come?"* Are you living for your Lord and for those descendants that will come after you? Our approach to life and efforts during this life significantly determine the extent of divine blessing will receive in the future.

All men were created by GOD. All men will die. All men will be called upon to pass through the veil. But only a few, only a few special men, only those who have been worthy to do the will of GOD, are given the honor to see GOD in paradise.

"I have told you these things, so that in me you may have peace. In this world you will have trouble. But take heart! I have overcome the world."- John 16:33 (NIV)

And in this life, especially in these times, all of us will go through some sort of tests that will require some sacrifice. When, or in what manner that sacrifice may be required, only GOD knows. Yours may be different from mine. All we can do is to pray for the grace so that when the time comes, we will be ready to complete the task that GOD gives without disappointing Him, so that when it is over, when we have done all we could, we might look to our Lord Jesus Christ and say the same words that Apostle Paul said

"I have fought the good fight, I have finished the race, I have kept the faith."- 2 Timothy 4:7 (NIV)

The Bible says Genesis 49:3-4 in *"Reuben, you are my firstborn, my might, the first sign of my strength, excelling in honor, excelling in power. Turbulent as the waters, you will no longer excel, for you went up onto your father's bed, onto my couch and defiled it."*

Jacob the son of Isaac stepped up and drilled his sons between the eyes. Previously, he was a passive, sissified father, but in his final days he stepped up. As parents, one of the things we must do is tell our children the truth. Our modern society has been caught up in self-esteem. We don't want to say or do anything that will jeopardize anyone's sense of worth.

From the culture I grew up in Yoruba, one of the three largest ethnic groups in Nigeria. The Yoruba language has an extensive literature of poetry, short stories and proverbs. The Yoruba people believe in showing the utmost respect to elders (elders meaning parents and their peers, grandparents, older friends and teachers). The Yoruba culture looks at the long term of a child. It spells out expectation ahead of time in order to protect family's good name. Healthy people are disciplined to be a better citizen.

> *"You said in your heart, "I will ascend to the heavens; I will raise my throne above the stars of God; I will sit enthroned on the mount of assembly, on the utmost heights of Mount Zaphon."*- Isaiah 14:13 (NIV)

Satan happened to be most rebellious and prideful being that has ever lived. He has always sought to have his own way. Apart from the boundaries GOD has placed upon him, he does whatever he wants. He hasn't turned out very well- Satan fell from glory and will end in ashes.

Parents, discipline your children according to the Bible. Exercise tough love. You may feel like your children are rascal (little devil) right now. Well, just wait. If you choose not to discipline them and speak frank and hard words, you will find that they will become menaces to society.

From the above passage, Reuben holds a special place in his father's heart by virtue of the fact that he was the firstborn. The firstborn son normally had two rights. First, he became the leader of the family. Second, he was entitled to a double share of the inheritance. But Reuben was not to receive this blessing because he was "uncontrolled as water."

The word translated "uncontrolled" means "anger or reckless or destructive". One of the things that GOD made me to understand was that anyone that cannot control his or her anger will have a limited GOD's power. He was teaching me that anger with the Power of GOD is destructive.

Anger is one of the deadly sins that men struggle with the most. Unfortunately, both sins can be handed down from generation to generation. Take anger, for example. It's interesting that Moses was a descendant of Levi. What problem kept Moses from beginning his divine work at first that made his assignment to be delayed for 40 years and then prevent Moses from entering the Promised Land? Anger!

> *"Looking this way and that and seeing no one, he killed the Egyptian and hid him in the sand."*- Exodus 2:12 (NIV)

Moses got angry and murdered the Egyptian who was mistreating the Hebrews and had to flee to the desert for 40 years.

> *"Take the staff, and you and your brother Aaron gather the assembly together. Speak to that rock before their eyes and it will pour out its water. You will bring water out of the rock for the community so they and their livestock can drink."*- Numbers 20:8 (NIV)

Then he got angry with the people and struck the rock to bring forth water, when GOD had told him to speak to the rock. For that sin, GOD prevented Moses from entering Canaan.

> *"Then Moses raised his arm and struck the rock twice with his staff. Water gushed out, and the community and their livestock drank."*- Numbers 20:11 (NIV)

Study of Reuben's life reflects an undisciplined life and indulgence.

> *" While Israel was living in that region, Reuben went in and slept with his father's concubine Bilhah, and Israel heard of it. Jacob had twelve sons"*- Genesis 35:22 (NIV)

The sins of the past disqualified Reuben from blessing of the future. From the above verse, after Rachel death Reuben slept with Rachel's servant—the mother of his brothers Dan and Naphtali. All the text tells us that Jacob heard about it. We don't know for certain why Reuben did this. This incident happened 40 years ago. Reuben, the firstborn, should have received a double portion of the inheritance. He should have been the leader among his brothers. He should be above all his brothers, should have been the one to defend his father's honor, not defile it. But his one act of indulgence robbed him of his privileges as the firstborn. Like King David after him, he paid a terrible price for a night of pleasure. One night of pleasure can destroy labor of lifetime.

One of the lessons from this Pastor's corner is that our actions today can determine our future blessings in GOD's program and the choices we make today will affect our descendants for generations to come. We must learn from Reuben we cannot afford to live recklessly. GOD, the righteous judge sees everything.

" For we must all appear before the judgment seat of Christ, so that each of us may receive what is due us for the things done while in the body, whether good or bad."- 2 Corinthians 5:10 (NIV)

Though we are secure in Christ, there are still consequences to our actions. We must continually recognize that one day we will have to give an account.

All the potential in the world won't benefit you if you don't develop self-control, especially in the area of sexual temptation. Satan can wait for lifetime for a believer to fall. He just sets his traps and bides his time.

You may be preeminent in dignity, power and full of anointing. But if you are as uncontrolled as water, it's only a matter of time until your potential is swept away by the flood of lust. You may have tremendous potential in the Lord. But you have got a habit of flowing downstream with lustful thoughts. It' is all in your head at this point. No one else knows and no one has gotten hurt or is a victim yet. It is better for you to stop it.

Great gifts are worthless without godly character.

I know many gifted pastors who are out of the ministry or lose their respect because they did not judge their lust or anger. If you aren't learning to take every thought captive to the obedience of Jesus Christ, it's only a matter of time before your great potential is ruined by reckless lust or anger. Reuben provides a gripping illustration that the passion of uncontrolled lust leads to ruin.

Let us look at the life of Reuben and his descendants after Jacob's prophecy:

Reubenites built an imposing altar of worship

> *"When they came to Geliloth near the Jordan in the land of Canaan, the Reubenites, the Gadites and the half-tribe of Manasseh built an imposing altar there by the Jordan."*- Joshua 22:10 (NIV)

Among other tribes so we know little about Reuben. The tribe produced no significant man, no judge, no king, and no prophet. The behavior of Reuben affects the destiny of his descendants.

The Bible says Deuteronomy 33:6, NIV - *"Let Reuben live and not die, nor his people be few."* You might be reading this Pastor's Corner and some people who have been fathers or mothers or mentors to you educationally, professionally, spiritually, or even biologically might have spoken a curse into your lives. Some did it without knowing but some did it deliberately. I am praying today and in this season that curse will be taken out by the Blood of Jesus and in the Mighty Name of Jesus. How do I know that the curse will be removed? From the Word of GOD that is greater than any curse or whosoever must have issued against you.

> *"Can plunder be taken from warriors, or captives be rescued from the fierce? But this is what the LORD says: "Yes, captives will be taken from warriors, and plunder retrieved from the fierce; I will contend*

with those who contend with you, and your children I will save." - Isaiah 49:24-25 (NIV)

GOD was reversing the curse that Jacob had put upon his first born, Reuben. Moses looked at the children of Israel and noticed that since the day Israel cursed Reuben, Reuben began to struggle and his tribe was diminishing. So Moses stood in authority and reversed the curse. Moses said 'let Reuben live'. Meaning Reuben was going slowly but surely to extinction.

I am praying for you today that you will live and you will not be few anymore in the Mighty name of Jesus. By the grace of GOD, GOD has given me grace to minister to you through this book, as Moses reversed it for Reuben; every curse in your marriage, ministry, health, prosperity and life shall be reversed in the Mighty Name of Jesus.

"Jesus said to her, "I am the resurrection and the life. The one who believes in me will live, even though they die; and whoever lives by believing in me will never die. Do you believe this?" - John 11:25–26 (NIV)

What the above passage meant was that Jesus Christ had paid the penalty by bearing the curse on the cross (Galatians 3:13) for everyone who will trust His word over Satan's or their own understanding. And everyone who believes in Jesus Christ will be raised from the dead just as Jesus Christ was resurrected (1 Corinthians 15:52–53, paraphrase).

Chapter Twenty-Five:
Take Caution

"But God said to me, 'You are not to build a house for my Name, because you are a warrior and have shed blood.'" - 1 Chronicles 28:3 (NIV)

King David has become king of both Judah and Israel. He has, in large measure, consolidated his kingdom. He has taken Jebus and made it his capital city, renaming it Jerusalem. He has built his palace and given thought to build a temple- a plan GOD significantly revises. But why would GOD revise His plan in building a temple for Him.

"One evening David got up from his bed and walked around on the roof of the palace. From the roof, he saw a woman bathing. The woman was very beautiful"- 2 Samuel 11: 2 (NIV)

King David has done battle with the Ammonites and prevailed, but he has not yet completely defeated them. The Ammonites have retreated to the royal city of Rabbah, and as the time for war approaches, King David sends all Israel, led by Joab, to besiege the city and to bring about its surrender.

King David has chosen not to endure the rigors of camping in the open field, outside the city. He has chosen to remain in Jerusalem. Sleeping late, David rises from his bed as others prepare to go to bed for the night. David strolls about the rooftop of his palace and happens to steal a look at a beautiful young woman bathing herself, perhaps ceremonially, in fulfillment of the law.

> *"and David sent someone to find out about her. The man said, "She is Bathsheba, the daughter of Eliam and the wife of Uriah the Hittite."* Then David sent messengers to get her. She came to him, and he slept with her"- 2 Samuel 11: 3-4 (NIV)

It was not due to any intent on the part of Bathsheba, nor even any indiscretion. She was bathing herself as darkness fell and being poor. She did not have the privilege of complete privacy, especially when the king could look down from the lofty heights of his rooftop vantage point. King David was struck with her beauty and sent messengers to inquire about her identity. They informed David of her identity, and that she was married to Uriah, the Hittite. That should have ended his interest, but it did not. David sent messengers who took her, bringing her to his palace, and there he sleeps with her. When she cleanses herself, she went home.

> *" The woman conceived and sent word to David, saying, "I am pregnant."* - 2 Samuel 11: 5 (NIV)

It all seems to be over. King David was not looking for another wife; he was not even looking for an affair. He was looking for a conquest. That should have happened on the battlefield, not in the bedroom. Things took a very different turn when Bathsheba sent word to the King that she was pregnant.

"So David sent this word to Joab: "Send me Uriah the Hittite." And Joab sent him to David. When Uriah came to him, David asked him how Joab was, how the soldiers were and how the war was going. Then David said to Uriah, "Go down to your house and wash your feet." So

Uriah left the palace, and a gift from the king was sent after him."- 2 Samuel 11: 6-8 (NIV).

King David first seeks to cover up his sin by ordering Joab to send Uriah home on furlough, ostensibly to give King David a report on the war. King David's efforts to get Uriah into bed with Bathsheba began as subtle hints, then changed to veiled orders, and then turned crass as King David seeks to get Uriah to do drunk what he will not do sober.

> *"Uriah said to David, "The ark and Israel and Judah are staying in tents,[a] and my commander Joab and my lord's men are camped in the open country. How could I go to my house to eat and drink and make love to my wife? As surely as you live, I will not do such a thing!"*
> - 2 Samuel 11: 11 (NIV).

When King David efforts fail to have Uriah to sleep with his wife, due to Uriah's noble character, David sends Uriah back to Joab, with written orders to Joab to put him to death in a way that makes it seem like a casualty of war. Joab does as he was asked and sent word to David: "Mission accomplished."

> The Bible says in Psalm 32:3-4, NIV - *"When I kept silent, my bones wasted away through my groaning all day long. For day and night your hand was heavy on me; my strength was sapped as in the heat of summer"*.

The above verses made it clear that King David was divinely prepared for repentance. King David made it clear that GOD was at work even when it does not appear to be so. During the time David tries to cover up his sin, GOD was at work exposing it in his heart. These are not times of pleasure and joy, as Satan would like us to collude; they are days of misery. David was plagued with guilt. He could not sleep, and it seems he could not eat. Whether or not King David recognizes it as GOD who was at work in him, he did know he was miserable. It was this misery which tenderizes David, preparing him for the rebuke Prophet Nathan was to bring, preparing him for repentance. David's repentance was not the result of David's assessment of his situation; it is the result of divine intervention. He has gone so far in sin that he could not think straight. GOD was at work in David's life to break him, so that he will once again cast himself upon GOD for grace.

"Then Nathan said to David, "You are the man! This is what the LORD, the God of Israel, says: 'I anointed you king over Israel, and I delivered you from the hand of Saul. I gave your master's house to you, and your master's wives into your arms. I gave you all Israel and Judah. And if all this had been too little, I would have given you even more. Why did you despise the word of the LORD by doing what is evil in his eyes? You struck down Uriah the Hittite with the sword and took his wife to be your own. You killed him with the sword of the Ammonites."- 2 Samuel 12: 7-9 (NIV)

Let's look at what GOD had done for King David:

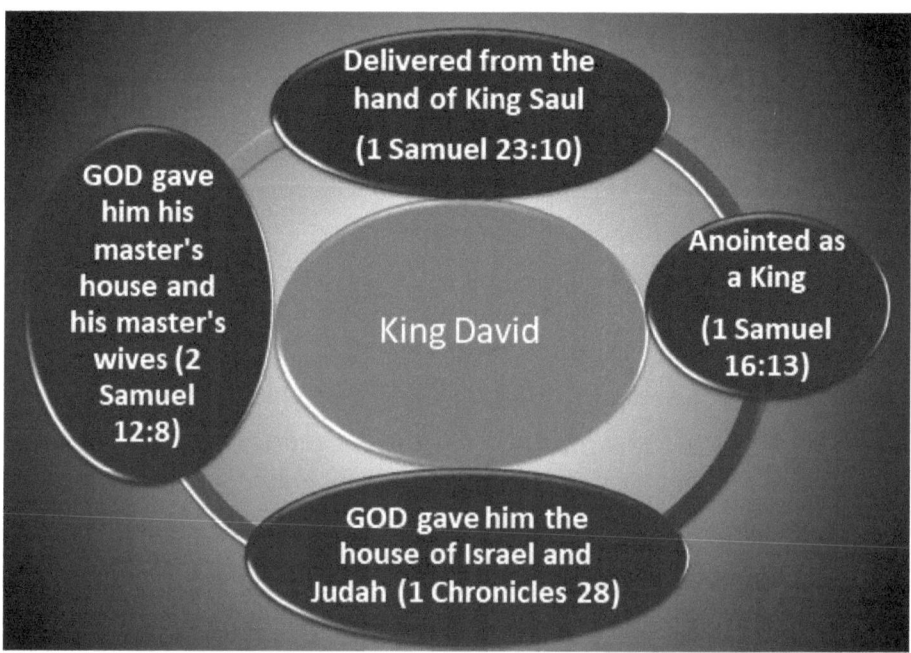

GOD spoke to David as though he has forgotten what he had done for him, or rather as though he has come to take credit for them himself. Everything David possesses has been given to him by GOD. Has it been so long since David was a lowly shepherd boy that he has forgotten? King David was a "rich" man because GOD has made him rich. And if he does not think he was rich enough, GOD would have given him more. King David had begun to cling to his "riches," rather than to cling to the GOD who made him rich.

King David does commit a sexual sin when he takes Bathsheba and sleeps with her, knowing she is a married woman. But this sexual sin is symptomatic, according to Nathan, and thus according to GOD. GOD was not just saying, "Shame on you, David. Look at all the wives and concubines you had to sleep with. And if none of these women pleased you, you could have obtained another woman, just one that was not already married.

"Against you, you only, have I sinned and done what is evil in your sight; so you are right in your verdict and justified when you judge." – Psalm 51: 4 (NIV)

First and foremost, David's sin was against GOD. He had ceased to humbly acknowledge GOD as the Giver of all he possessed. He had ceased to look to GOD to provide him with all his needs and his desires. David had not only ceased to ask GOD to supply his needs, but he had also disobeyed GOD's commands by committing adultery and murder. David's sin against GOD manifests itself by the evils he committed against others.

"This is what the LORD says: 'Out of your own household I am going to bring calamity on you. Before your very eyes I will take your wives and give them to one who is close to you, and he will sleep with your wives in broad daylight. You did it in secret, but I will do this thing in broad daylight before all Israel." - 2 Samuel 12: 11-12 (NIV)

Nathan outlined these sins, employing a repetitive *"you:"*

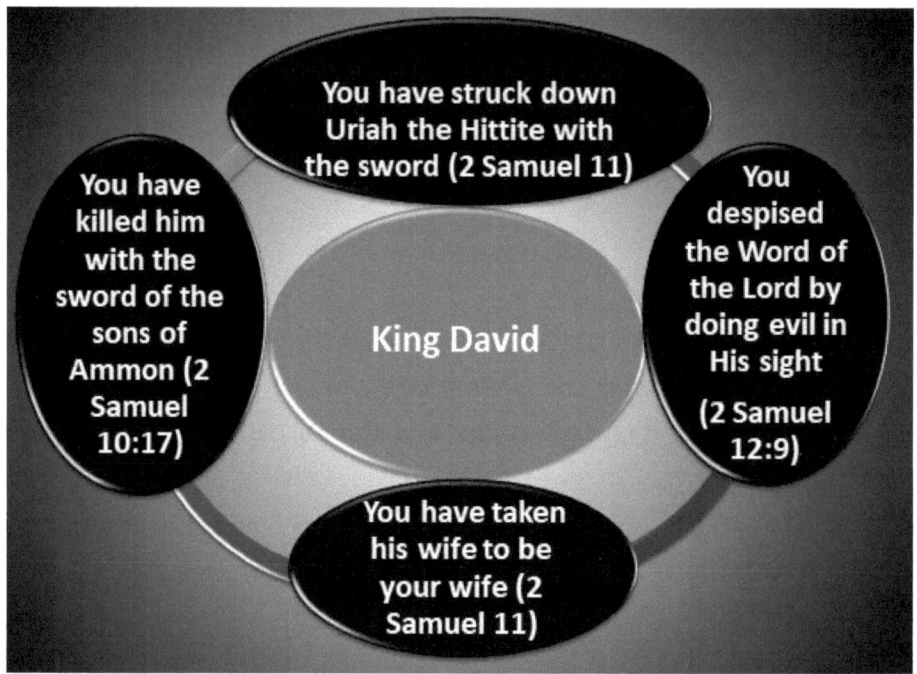

The consequences are not only appropriate but intensified. David as King took one man's wife; another will take several of his wives. This happens when Absalom rebels against his father's rule and temporarily takes over the throne. Following the advice of Ahithophel, Absalom pitches a tent on the roof of David's palace (the place from which David first looked upon Bathsheba) and there, in the sight of all Israel, slept with King David's concubines as a declaration that he has taken over his father's throne and all that goes with it.

The Bible says in Psalm 73: 11, NIV - *"They say, "How would God know? Does the Most High know anything?"*

GOD may delay judgment or discipline, but He will never ignore our sin. GOD is under no obligation to stop us from sinning. Sometimes people justify their sin by saying something like: *"I have prayed about it and asked GOD to stop me if it is a wrong."*

When GOD does not stop them, they somehow assume it must be right. GOD could have stopped King David after he chose to stay home from the war, or after he began to covet Uriah's wife, or after he committed adultery, but instead, He allowed David to persist in his sin for some time.

As Yoruba people in West Africa will say *"oju apa,ko le jo oju ara"*. The translation is that *"a body with a scar would never be the same"*.

GOD even allowed David to get away with murder, for a time but it prevented King David from building a temple for GOD. David's sin, like all sin, is never worth the price and eventual consequence.

The Gospel of Jesus Christ is *"Good News."* The *"Good News"* is that the death of our Lord, which reveals the immensity of our sin, is the immense work of GOD by which He can and will forgive us of our sin. By His innocent and sacrificial death, Jesus died in our place, paid the penalty for our sins. He bore our sins on the cross! And by trusting in His death, burial, and resurrection, we die to sin and are raised to newness of eternal life, in Christ.

Chapter Twenty-Six: Remain Focus

"The LORD replied, "My Presence will go with you, and I will give you rest"- Exodus 33:14 (NIV)

When Moses arrived a point in his journey of life, he realized that the best education, training, and skills he acquired in Pharaoh's court to be a successful leader and his abilities alone were not adequate to lead a people to GOD's desired destiny. He was ready to give up. It was too hard for him to proceed. The people fell into idol worship. The people became obstinate. His skill sets were not adequate for the enormous mission that GOD had committed to him.

"Then Moses said to him, "If your Presence does not go with us, do not send us up from here."- Exodus 33:15 (NIV)

"I cannot go on like this". He asked for GOD''s help. And GOD spoke, **"My Presence will go with you, and I will give you rest."** Each of us must get to this realization if we are to experience the full purpose of our life. Life lessons has taught me that there are every tendencies to give up when circumstances seem impossible, when all signs of grace seem at their lowest ebb, when the fragmenting effect of multiple pressures seems relentless. When temptation is fiercest, when love and joy and hope seem well-nigh extinguished in heart.

My brothers and sisters, I am encouraging you today, do not give up as you labor sincerely in obscurity and you wonder how much it even matters. I want you to know that our Heavenly Father who sees in secret will reward you very soon. (Matthew 6:4, paraphrase). Remain focus on GOD who is not only powerful and supreme; He is also dependable, for He never fails. The Word says that GOD keeps His covenant up to a thousand generations. He will remember you today in the Mighty Name of Jesus.

Your real life is not about your achievement. Your life begins with GOD. A fulfilled life surrenders to GOD to fulfill His plan, not us trying to use GOD for our own personal ambition. The deepest level of appreciation to your maker is to praise HIM in spite of the pain and hardship you are through now, thanking HIM during those trials, trust HIM to deliver you, and love GOD the more as HE seems distant from you.

The Bible says in Psalm 16:11, NIV -" **You make known to me the path of life; you will fill me with joy in your presence, with eternal pleasures at your right hand.**" There are no shortcuts to joy than be in GOD's Presence. Joy is different from happiness. Happiness is based on circumstances but joy is based on GOD. Happiness is like the moon, waxing and waning. Joy is like the sun, always shining even when night falls or clouds cover it. Happiness is like exchanging seasonal gifts and decorating our house for Christmas; joy is the awareness of what Christmas is all about. The presence of the Lord brings to one unspeakable joy, that's joy that is almost impossible to describe adequately in words. This joy derived from GOD's Presence transcends beyond the boundaries of this present life. You cannot derive that joy outside GOD because you were made for a mission. The overall mission is to have a ministry in the Body of Christ and a mission to propagate the gospel in the world. As long as you are walking in the path of righteousness, satan is seeking daily to distract in order to obstruct you - he will utilize various tactics and mercenaries. Just be focus and prayerful, the Lord shall give you victory over lucifer in the Mighty Name of Jesus. Amen.

GOD has designed this planet, earth to be a temporary residence for us; it is extremely brief at most 150 years. It cannot be compared to billions of years in eternity. You would not be here long, so do not get too attached to this world. GOD has ordained a destination for you; Heaven has nothing to do with your material abundance. You came to this world with nothing; you are not leaving with anything.

The journey to that life eternity with GOD in Heaven starts when you sincerely humbling accept Jesus Christ as your Lord and Savior. Jesus Christ declared:

"Jesus answered, "I am the way and the truth and the life. No one comes to the Father except through me." - John 14:6 (NIV).

He is not saying that He is one among many ways; He is saying that He is the one and only way. Humbling accepting Jesus Christ today is not putting yourself down or denying your strengths; rather, it is being honest about your weaknesses and the fact about your present situation.

Chapter Twenty-Seven: Winning is Crucial

"How you have fallen from heaven, O star of the morning, son of the dawn! You have been cut down to the earth, You who have weakened the nations! "But you said in your heart, 'I will ascend to heaven; I will raise my throne above the stars of God, And I will sit on the mount of assembly In the recesses of the north. 'I will ascend above the heights of the clouds; I will make myself like the Most High". – Isaiah 14:12-14 (NIV)

It is clear from these verses that Prophet Isaiah was speaking of someone possessing some power. He was speaking of none other than satan. He was the angel who was created by GOD.

"You were in Eden, the garden of God; every precious stone adorned you: carnelian, chrysolite and emerald, topaz, onyx and jasper, lapis lazuli, turquoise and beryl. Your settings and mountings were made of gold; on the day you were created they were prepared."- Ezekiel 28:13 (NIV)

He was given the highest authority under GOD, but was not content with this. He was the one who was in Eden, the garden of GOD. He was once blameless at the time of his creation, but then was found with sin (Ezekiel 28:15, paraphrase). He possessed great beauty, power, and authority, but he had to have more. He wanted to exalt himself further; he wanted to become like GOD (Isaiah 14:14, paraphrase).

It is apparent that satan is the enemy of GOD, and that he actively seeks to oppose GOD's purposes and people. Our Lord Jesus Christ mentioned satan as the source of temptation and trials in the Body of Christ. I am also inclined to believe that satan was not only trying to make a point with GOD, but with his fellow-angels and agents ever seeking to cause believers to stumble and attempting to thwart the plans and purposes of GOD for our lives as the children of GOD.

We are engaged in the spiritual warfare, and our number one enemy is Satan and a host of unseen angelic and celestial enemies whose power vastly exceeds ordinary human's power. These enemies remain invisible to our eyes, but they nevertheless are real, and so are their attacks. All genuine believers are constantly on satan's radar of attack in order to distract us, and thereby cut us off from our source of power and protection which is the GOD Almighty. These celestial enemies seem to have various forms, as is suggested by the variety of terms "rulers," "powers," "world forces of darkness," or "spiritual forces of wickedness in the heavenly places". I hope this book opens your eyes to fully grasp the variety and the number of those forces which are opposing us.

> The Bible says in Ephesians 6: 13, NIV – **"Therefore put on the full armor of God, so that when the day of evil comes, you may be able to stand your ground, and after you have done everything, to stand"**.

Our protection against these forces is assured only if and when we take up the full armor of GOD. The full armor of GOD includes the truth which is easy to understand, since satan is said to be the **"father of lies"**.

Winston Churchill (1874-1965) once said

"The truth is incontrovertible. Malice may attack it, ignorance may deride it, but in the end, there it is".

Deception is high on the list of things GOD considers to be an abomination. A "lying tongue" is one of the things He describes as "detestable to Him" (Proverbs 6:16-17, paraphrase). Believers should desist from telling lies against one another like politicians to minimize the attack of the enemies against the Body of Christ- the Church.

The full armor of GOD also includes the sword of the Spirit, which is the Word of GOD- the Bible. While all the other pieces of spiritual armor are defensive in nature, the sword of the Spirit is the only offensive weapon in the armor of GOD. The Word of GOD speaks of the holiness and the power of GOD. A greater spiritual weapon is conceivable in the Word of GOD, what a blessing that the same Word is available to us today and forever. The Word of GOD defeats the powers of darkness. The Word of GOD must be study every day, we must meditate in it every time, it must be mixed with faith to be active, and we must use it. Any believers that failed to apply the Word of GOD will not last very long. Our Lord, Jesus Christ used the sword of the Spirit during temptation in the wilderness (Matthew 4:1-11). Every time the devil came at our Lord Jesus Christ, He drew His sword and used it. Because of this the devil left Him for a time (Luke 4:13, paraphrase).

"Moses answered the people, "Do not be afraid. Stand firm and you will see the deliverance the Lord will bring you today. The Egyptians you see today you will never see again. 14 The Lord will fight for you; you need only to be still." - Exodus 14: 13-14 (NIV).

When we engaged in the battle, it is the GOD Almighty, the most powerful; the ONE who had never lost any battle that will fight those battles and give us victory. When David fought Goliath, he did not even have a sword, but only a sling. While David fought, it was the Lord who gave the victory. Even Goliath's pronouncement to David made it clear that this young man could not prevail on his own. And David's words made it clear that the battle and the victory was the Lord's. If you are going through an intensive battle, the LORD himself will fight for you. Just stay calm.

I want to encourage you to stay focus on GOD and believe that He is with you, fight those battle on your knees, don't give up, put on full armor of GOD, worship GOD to invite His Presence, and victory is certain because the battle is already won before it started The race has already been run for you. It is done; you just have to claim your victory today. No matter how bad a situation is, GOD can bring something good from it. Something good is coming out of that hopeless situation you are in, if only you stay focus on GOD and His promises. You shall be victorious in the Mighty Name of Jesus.

Chapter Twenty-Eight: The Road To Victory

"For we who are alive are always being given over to death for Jesus' sake, so that his life may also be revealed in our mortal body." - 2 Corinthians 4:11 (NIV)

Almost everyone, particularly in the ministry must endure considerable rejection and misunderstanding. We must learn to overcome rejection and misunderstanding by forgiving and praying for our persecutors just as the Lord Jesus Christ did for those who nailed Him to the cross. This is essential if we are genuinely born again; walk in the Spirit and for us to be able to exercise true spiritual authority. We must come to the level of maturity where the love of Jesus Christ controls us, to love people who hate us and forgive them.

"For Christ's love compels us, because we are convinced that one died for all, and therefore all died." - 2 Corinthians 5:14 (NIV)

Love does not take into account the wrongs we have suffered, and is not motivated by rejection, which drives us to retaliate or try to prove ourselves. Such reactions can slide us away from the spiritual authority that GOD has provided for us through His Son, Jesus Christ. Learning to deal with rejection, political maneuvering, jealousy, gossip, back stabbing, insinuation and misunderstanding is mandatory if we are to fulfill

GOD's plan for our life. At times, GOD allow these as a form of discipline in order for us to grow in grace and die a little more to ambition, pride, and other motives which so quickly stain our revelation or testimony. GOD allow those circumstances for us to depend solely on Him alone, and to know more of His grace and power to deliver us from those situations or powers that seem to be too much for us to handle. If we stand against the discipline from GOD we might slide into the darkness.

"Fear of man will prove to be a snare, but whoever trusts in the Lord is kept safe"- Proverbs 29:25 (NIV)

King Saul is a good example of how a man that started well with GOD, someone with a true commission from GOD can slide away from the light of GOD. When he was commanded to wait for Prophet Samuel before offering the sacrifice, he succumbed to pressure and offered it prematurely.

"What have you done?" asked Samuel. Saul replied, *"When I saw that the men were scattering, and that you did not come at the set time, and that the Philistines were assembling at Mikmash"* - 1 Samuel 13:11 (NIV)

When we begin to fear the people, or magnify the circumstances more than GOD we might open door for the devil and wrath of GOD. Those who have relationship with the devil are trapped - fear has snared them.

Anything built with hype, manipulation or control spirits cannot last long. Those who are caught in this deadly trap of devil will fear those who walk in the true power and anointing of GOD. This is because those who walk in true spiritual authority are the least affected by the manipulation or spirit of control. Compared to the power of GOD, all the power of the evil one cannot even register on the scale.

> *"Against whom has the king of Israel come out? Who are you pursuing? A dead dog? A flea?"*- 1 Samuel 24:14 (NIV)

For instance, King Saul was very mad with David and even consumed to destroy him despite the fact that David was nobody - regarded to as *"a flea"*. As the manipulation and control spirits increase their dominion, so will the paranoia of those who are trapped in their grasp. Such people will unreasonably consume with passion to destroy or stain anyone who threatens their authority or control.

> *"Then it goes and takes with it seven other spirits more wicked than itself, and they go in and live there. And the final condition of that person is worse than the first. That is how it will be with this wicked generation."*- Mathew 12:45 (NIV).

Anyone that GOD has provided with power and authority must be aware that they will be the primary targets of devil and his agents, and if such individual rebel against Holy Spirit, the void will be filled by the counterfeit spiritual authority of darkness.

> *"Then the king ordered the guards at his side: "Turn and kill the priests of the LORD, because they too have sided with David. They knew he was fleeing, yet they did not tell me." But the king's officials were unwilling to raise a hand to strike the priests of the LORD."*- 1 Samuel 22:17 (NIV)

This may begin as simple persecuting those who are faithful to the Lord. King Saul killed the true priests and spent one of his last days in the house of a woman with a familiar spirit (1 Samuel 28:7).

> *"Again, the devil took him to a very high mountain and showed him all the kingdoms of the world and their splendor. All this I will give you,"* he said, *"if you will bow down and worship me."*- Mathew 4:8-9 (NIV

Satan is always looking for opportunity to tempt everyone called by GOD with the same temptation he offered to our Lord Jesus Christ. As long as people are ready to bow down to satan, his ways and his agents, he is ready to promote them and give such people authority over his kingdom. Satan's strategy is to offer the quick and easy path to the same place to which GOD has called us.

"For our struggle is not against flesh and blood, but against the rulers, against the authorities, against the powers of this dark world and against the spiritual forces of evil in the heavenly realms" - Ephesians 6:12 (NIV)

Gossip, jealousy and political maneuvering can have some effect on Christians, if we allow ourselves to be manipulated by someone with a controlling spirit. We can be resentful or bitter toward that person. In such a case, the enemy can cause us to fall and open doors for discouragement, disorientation and depression spirits. Unless, we have learned to bless those who curse us as the Lord Jesus Christ commanded. This does not mean that we bless their works, but that we pray for them and not against them. If such people with control spirit can get us to retaliate, they will have us using the same spirit, and we might multiplied the very evil we were trying to forbid or cast out.

The Bible says in 1 Kings 19:1-2, NIV -"***Now Ahab told Jezebel everything Elijah had done and how he had killed all the prophets with the sword. So Jezebel sent a messenger to Elijah to say***, *"May the gods deal with me, be it ever so severely, if by this time tomorrow I do not make your life like that of one of them."*

Elijah had just had a mountaintop experience or a major victory in defeating the prophets of Baal on Mount Carmel. The fire from the Lord came down and burned the sacrifice, the people had acknowledged the true Living GOD, and the false prophets were all put to death (1 Kings 18:38-40). But that experience was followed by an episode of fear and failure in Elijah's life, the prophet was afraid and ran for his life from Jezebel.

> *"But he himself went a day's journey into the wilderness, and came and sat down under a [a]broom tree. And he prayed that he might die, and said, "It is enough! Now, Lord, take my life, for I am no better than my fathers."*- 1 Kings 19:4 (NKJV)

The death threat caused Elijah to flee a day's journey into the wilderness. At one point Elijah was so discouraged that he desired to die. Everyone gets discouraged at times and it can be for many different reasons. You might even be discouraged today. Discouragement never comes from GOD. Discouragement is, in fact, the very opposite of love, joy, peace and other attributes of the fruits of Holy Spirit (Galatians 5:22-23, paraphrase).

Many people get discouraged or angry for no apparent reason, which can be traced to the darkness. When your situations or difficulties seem insurmountable and you want to give up, even those situations are not really more than usual, you are probably coming under spiritual attack.

Discouragement is meant to weaken you for the next level of attack and assault by satan. You need to be aware of the operations of darkness.

> *"For our light affliction, which is but for a moment, is working for us a far more exceeding and eternal weight of glory, while we do not look at the things which are seen, but at the things which are not seen. For the things which are seen are temporary, but the things which are not seen are eternal."*. - 2 Cor. 4:17-18 (NKJV)

No sensible person will fight to win if they do not believe victory is possible. Anything you are going through right now, pains you are feeling, disappointment and discouragement are momentary defeat which would eventually accomplish the purposes of GOD, and also serves as a prelude to satan's final destruction. You need to tenaciously resist the works of darkness and hold on to GOD to release His Presence into your life.

"And they overcame him by the blood of the Lamb and by the word of their testimony, and they did not love their lives to the death."- Revelation 12:11 (NKJV)

We overcome by the Blood of the Lamb as we take our stand on what our Heavenly Father and His Son, Jesus Christ has already accomplished for us. The battle is already won for us, the road to victory is opened and the victory is certain, and there is no way we can lose if we abide in Him.

The Bible says in Exodus 14: 13-14, NKJV -" And Moses said to the people, *"Do not be afraid. Stand still, and see the salvation[a] of the Lord, which He will accomplish for you today. For the Egyptians whom you see today, you shall see again no more forever. 14 The Lord will fight for you, and you shall hold[b] your peace."* When the Christian is actively engaged in the battle, it is the Lord who wins the victory. Our Lord Jesus Christ spoke of satan's defeat a number of times in the Gospels. In every instance, His defeat is viewed as accomplished at the Cross of Calvary. Our salvation and satan's defeat has already been accomplished by our Lord, when He died on the Cross of Calvary and then rose from the dead, triumphing over His foes, foremost of whom is satan himself and his works.

Our defenses and victory are directly tied to the Word of GOD in the Bible. They are truth, righteousness, the preparation of the gospel of peace, the shield of faith, the helmet of salvation, the Blood of Jesus, our testimony and the Word of GOD. Our deliverance from satan's power and our defense from his subsequent attacks are found in Jesus Christ and in the gospel which His death and resurrection have made a reality. The road to our victory is a matter of trusting and obeying our Lord.

When our life comes to an end, I pray that we will be able, like Apostle Paul, to say that I have fought the good fight, I have finished the course, I have kept the faith.

Chapter Twenty-Nine:
The Lord Shall Provide You With Strength To Overcome Temptation

"For God knows that when you eat from it your eyes will be opened, and you will be like God, knowing good and evil." - Genesis 3:5 (NKJV)

Temptation thrives on falsehood, deception, and evasion. Temptation and truth are rarely walked together. Temptation is selective about the facts it reveals, and most often it lies about the facts. Temptation tells men what they want to hear, not what they need to hear. It therefore minimizes the consequences of an evil act, minimizes the risk and maximizes the benefits. It promises the knowledge of good and evil, and it denies the penalty of death.

" Jesus answered, "My kingdom is not of this world. If My kingdom were of this world, My servants would fight, so that I should not be delivered to the Jews; but now My kingdom is not from here."- John 18:36 (NKJV)

Most politicians always telling voters what they want to hear, and then do nothing after they might have been elected into the office. During 2016 United States presidential election campaign, one candidate stated that he will make America great again. By bringing jobs back and building a wall between two countries, the candidate didn't tell that he will have the legislative branch to deal with. If the candidate is elected and his party loses two branches of Congress, he will have an uphill battle.

Another candidate was telling voters that the mission was to fight for the middle class. Of course, while the candidate was busy fundraising at almost $35,000 per plate. I wonder how many single middle-class people working that can afford that price. I wonder how many middle class will be in this candidate's cabinet assuming this candidate was elected.

"With flattery he will corrupt those who have violated the covenant, but the people who know their God will firmly resist him."- Daniel 11:32 (NIV)

Temptation proposes a shortcut or an easy way to reach our goals. Satan's temptations will propose some way in which man can meet his needs or goals, but with a lower price tag, with less pain and self-sacrifice.

"And he said to him, "I will give you all their authority and splendor; it has been given to me, and I can give it to anyone I want to. If you worship me, it will all be yours." - Luke 4:6-7 (NIV)

Temptation offers future rewards for today. In another words, it trades the future for the present, pleasure for pain, and the seen for the unseen. Temptation always seems to offer a big prize or juicy reward for a small price, just like the passage in the Luke 4: 6-7, kingdom for a mere bowing of the knee, but there is always a higher, hidden cost for anything you receive from satan and his kingdom of darkness. When you agree to satan's terms, he can give you fame, money, motivation, position, access or opportunities but he wouldn't tell you that those terms comes with hidden cost which you might not be able to negotiate with.

The Bible says in Luke 4:9, NIV -"***The devil led him to Jerusalem and had him stand on the highest point of the temple. "If you are the Son of God,"*** he said, *"throw yourself down from here."*

Temptation is frequently a solicitation to act promptly, immediately, hastily, without prayer, counsel, or deliberation. Every act which satan proposed to our Lord Jesus Christ to perform was an immediate one. In another words, every temptation which is described is a temptation to act now. For instances, our Lord Jesus Christ was commanded to turn the stone to become bread now. He was to bow down to Satan in worship, and thus receive his kingdom now. He was also urged jump from the pinnacle of the temple now. Ultimately, temptation is so unreasonable, and thus satan gives one little time to ponder his requests. All three of satan's temptations were based on a challenge that Jesus proves that He was the Son of GOD.

" Because he himself suffered when he was tempted, he is able to help those who are being tempted."- Hebrews 2:18 (NIV)

Temptation usually appeals to our lower motives, instincts and fears. Temptations appeals to the person who feels the need to prove something. Just like the life insurance agent will market insurance product if something happens. We should not need to be tempted to buy life insurance.

"For in the gospel the righteousness of God is revealed—a righteousness that is by faith from first to last,[a] just as it is written: "The righteous will live by faith." - Romans 1:17 (NIV)

A person should hardly require convincing concerning their responsibility to provide for their loved ones. It is the carnival, with its virtually useless goods and services which require the hawkers and barkers.

"Jesus answered, "I am the way and the truth and the life. No one comes to the Father except through me."- John 14:6 (NIV)

Temptation appeals to people's greed, but the Truth appeals to grace. Temptation appeals to lust, but the Truth appeals to love. Temptation appeals to death, but the Blood of Jesus and faith appeals to life and to give us abundant life as He promised us through His Word:

" The thief comes only to steal and kill and destroy; I have come that they may have life, and have it to the full."- John 10:10 (NIV)

The Bible says in Luke 4:32-34, NIV -" They were amazed at his teaching, because his words had authority. In the synagogue there was a man possessed by a demon, an impure spirit. He cried out at the top of his voice, *"Go away! What do you want with us, Jesus of Nazareth? Have you come to destroy us? I know who you are—the Holy One of God."*

Jesus Christ's victory over the temptations of satan had various implications and ramifications as reflect on the next page:

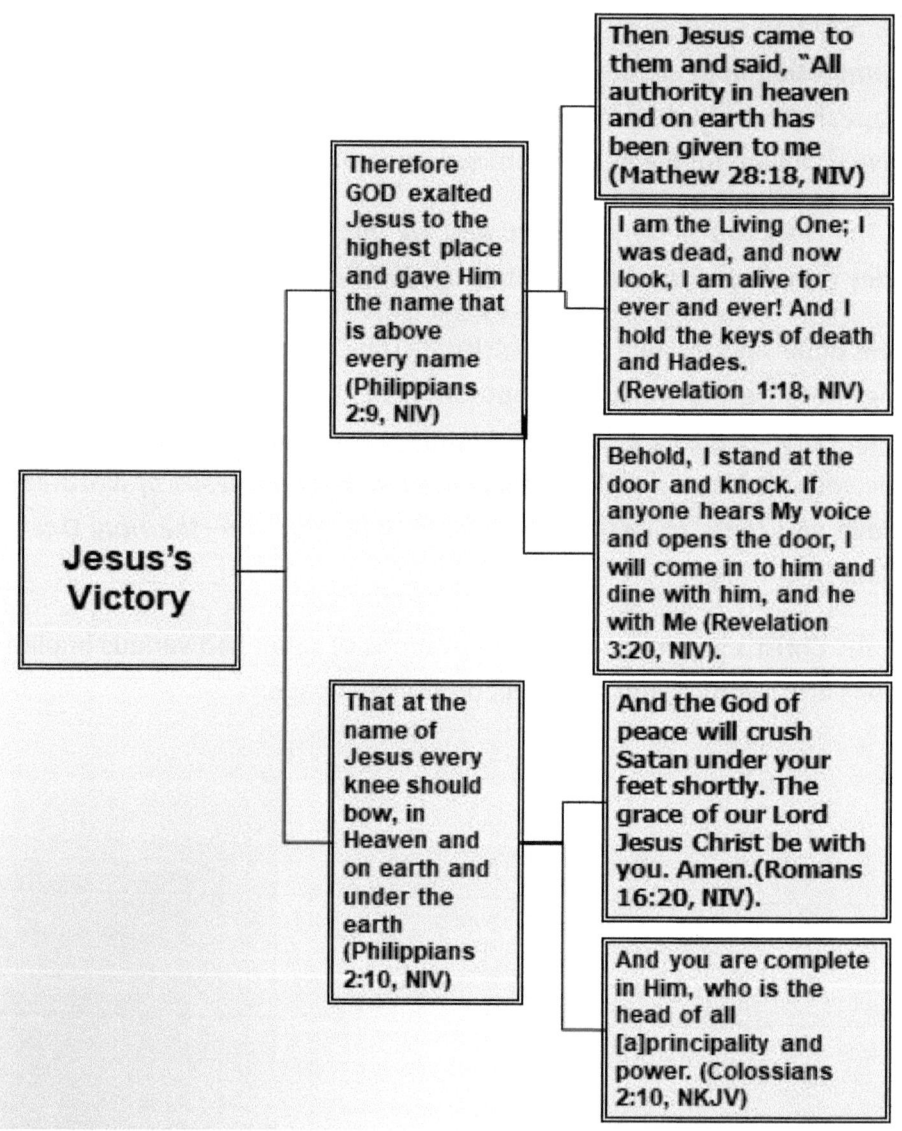

For Jesus Christ, emerging sinless from the temptations proved Him to be qualified as GOD's Son to rule over the earth. It further proved Him to be the Lamb of GOD, without spot, and thus made Him to be qualified to be our Lord and Savior who die for the sins of men. The temptation of our Lord Jesus Christ served to clarify and to intensify His sense of calling and direction. He came forth from His being tempted with full of the Spirit and power, and immediately began to proclaim the gospel of the Kingdom of GOD. In addition, He began to attack the kingdom of satan, casting out demons, and begin acknowledged as the Son of GOD by them. They even acknowledged that He had come to destroy them.

"if we endure, we will also reign with him. If we disown him, he will also disown us"- 2 Timothy 2:12 (NIV).

In the temptation Christ identified with mankind, with men and women in general. Likewise, if we can endure temptation as Jesus Christ did. He assured us that He will provide us with the power and ability to do the works He was doing while on earth and we will do even greater things than Him.

Chapter Thirty:
Be Cheerful, GOD Shall Give You Permanent Victory

"For our struggle is not against flesh and blood, but against the rulers, against the authorities, against the powers of this dark world and against the spiritual forces of evil in the heavenly realms."- Ephesians 6: 12 (NIV)

It should come as no surprise to us that we are engaged in a great spiritual battle. From the early chapters of the Old Testament it is apparent that satan is the enemy of GOD, and that he actively seeks to oppose GOD's purposes and GOD's people. Actually, the battle began long before you and I were formed in our mother's womb. Satan's rebellion against GOD was described in two Old Testament prophecies in Ezekiel 28:12-15, and below passage in Isaiah 14:12-14 (NIV):

"How you have fallen from heaven, morning star, son of the dawn! You have been cast down to the earth, you who once laid low the nations! You said in your heart, "I will ascend to the heavens; I will raise my throne above the stars of God; I will sit enthroned on the mount of assembly, on the utmost heights of Mount Zaphon.[a] I will ascend above the tops of the clouds; I will make myself like the Most High".

The war is not being waged to see which side will win. GOD has already won the war by the death of His Son, Jesus Christ on the cross of Calvary (John 12:31). In another words, the good news for the believers is that we are engaging in war that has already been won for us. The war is for our good, and for GOD's glory. This war is part of GOD's eternal plan and purpose for His creation.

The Bible says in 2 Corinthians 10:4 (NIV)- *"For the weapons of our warfare are not carnal, but mighty through God to the pulling down of strong holds"*. The weapons which GOD has provided us are those that best repel the attacks of satan. The weapons to defeat satan can be found only in Jesus Christ. Putting on the full armor of GOD is putting on the armor which our Lord utilized on the cross to bring about salvation. In another words, when we put on the full armor of GOD we are actually putting on Jesus Christ, the son of GOD. That's the reason, satan fears the name of Jesus, and the Blood of Jesus, but satan fears most the return of Jesus Christ for it will mark the end of satan's atrocities and influence on earth.

Therefore, it is imperative for everyone that wants to be victorious to strive to do only the things which would bring honor to Christ. If you are facing trial situations, don't allow them to rob you of your joy and victory, put on the full armor of GOD. The Bible tells us that *" God is our refuge and strength, an ever-present help in trouble."* (Psalms 46:1 NIV). You are not alone. Jesus has promised to never leave nor forsake us (Heb. 12:13). Turn your attention to Him and His Word. Wait upon Him and He will strengthen you with His peace. *"You will keep in perfect peace those whose minds are steadfast, because they trust in you."*- (Isaiah 26:3 NIV). By faith, release your cares, your concerns and worries to Him. Trust Him to work out the end result. He will either change your circumstance or will change you to deal with them. Claim and take His rest and peace upon you, believing that He has taken the burden from you. *"Cast all your anxiety on him because he cares for you."* - 1 Peter 5:7 (NIV).

The Bible says in 2 kings 6: 16, NIV -" ***"Don't be afraid,"*** the prophet answered. ***"Those who are with us are more than those who are with them."*** While Elisha's servant was terrified by what he had seen, Elisha remained calm. He knew something that his servant did not know. He knew that earthly armies were no threat when the host of Heaven was on his side. And so he prayed that the eyes of his servant might be opened, to see the *"invisible army"* which was on duty to protect the people of GOD. I want you to take a few minutes to worship and appreciate GOD now for the host of Heaven that's fighting our battle. GOD can never sleep nor slumber because of us. He has engraved us in the palm of His hand to demonstrate how He cares for us. When we are weak, He is around to make us strong. When we are lost, He will be our way. When we are discouraged, He is willing to encourage you. When it seems we have fallen, He will make us to rise again and even higher. When we are hurt, He will heal us completely. When you are broken, He is more than able to mend us permanently. Rejoice, those trials will soon be over, and you shall be victorious in Jesus' name. Amen.

Chapter Thirty-One: GOD Shall Deliver You From Ship-wreck

"The next day, because we were violently battered by the storm, they began throwing the cargo overboard, and on the third day they threw the ship's gear overboard with their own hands. When neither sun nor stars appeared for many days and a violent storm continued to batter us, we finally abandoned all hope of being saved." - Acts 27:18-20 (NIV)

The ship where Apostle Paul and other passengers were boarding was in a serious danger. Without warning, a hurricane-force wind blew down from the island. The winds were so strong, there was no nothing to do but allow the ship to be driven in the opposite direction from their heading. When the storm was just as relentless the next day, they began throwing the ship's cargo overboard. The storm continued to pound the ship and passengers for many days. Finally, all hope of being saved was defeated.

"And now I advise you to keep up your courage, for there will be no loss of life among you, but only the ship will be lost. For last night an angel of the God to whom I belong and whom I serve came to me and said, 'Do not be afraid, Paul! You must stand before Caesar, and God

> *has graciously granted you the safety of all who are sailing with you."*- Acts 27:22-24 (NIV)

An angel of GOD had appeared to Apostle Paul in the night, assuring him that all the passengers would be saved from the ravages of this storm. This was because the GOD Almighty was protecting Apostle Paul, who must stand before Caesar. It was because of Apostle Paul that his shipmates as well could survive the storm. No life would be lost, but only the ship, which would run aground on some island. Apostle Paul's shipmates should be encouraged by his faith in GOD, trusting that what GOD had promised, He would do.

> *"Just before dawn Paul urged them all to eat. "For the last fourteen days,"* he said, *"you have been in constant suspense and have gone without food—you haven't eaten anything."*- Acts 27:33 (NIV).

Two full weeks had passed, and the storm showed no sign of weakening. No one had seen the sun, the moon, or the stars for many days. The sailors had no idea where they were. The ship was being driven about at the mercy of the wind. All hope of survival was gone. When all human hope is gone, the stage has been set for our omnipotent GOD to intervene.

> *"And call upon me in the day of trouble: I will deliver thee, and thou shalt glorify me."*- Psalm 50:15 (NIV).

There are sobering times that we live in today. Many people have lost jobs and can't find one. Others are underemployed and are just barely making it. No one really knows the true unemployment rate since most people have left job market, the stock market is volatile, and there are severe unrests in most parts of the world. And with turmoil going on in the world people are becoming desperate and anxious; even the people of GOD.

GOD actually desires that we be utterly dependent upon Him as we are in desperate need of His help. Think of a human father. What good father would not want his children to turn to him when they need help? Naturally, a father loves it when his children come to him to seek help. There is something special about having someone there for you. GOD is this true source and He is more reliable than any human parents.

The Bible says in Philippians 1: 6, NIV – **"being confident of this, that he who began a good work in you will carry it on to completion until the day of Christ Jesus."**

If you are a Christian, GOD has a purpose for your life, and I can assure you right now as you are reading this book that GOD will ensure that it will be accomplished. What a comfort the Sovereignty of GOD is to the believer. It assures us that what GOD starts, GOD finishes against all odds.

> **"But the centurion wanted to spare Paul's life and kept them from carrying out their plan. He ordered those who could swim to jump overboard first and get to land. 44 The rest were to get there on planks or on other pieces of the ship. In this way everyone reached land safely."**- Acts 27:43-44 (NIV)

Later, Apostle Paul and other passengers were brought safely to the land. Apostle Paul was not anxious when he was in danger but encouraging others and he remained peaceful, even dreaming while others couldn't sleep or eat because he knows that it is GOD that promised to save them, and He will finish what He started.

> **"and through your offspring all nations on earth will be blessed, because you have obeyed me."**- Genesis 22:18 (NIV).

GOD promised Abram that He would give him and his wife Sarai a son, and that their descendants would possess the land of Canaan. When Abram fled to Egypt during the famine, he passed Sarai off as his sister.

GOD rescued Abram and Sarai from this situation because of the covenant He had made with Abram. He could not fulfill His covenant with Abram if Sarai became the wife of Pharaoh, nor could He do so if Pharaoh killed Abram for his deception. GOD spared Abram and Sarai in order to fulfill His promise. So also GOD spared Apostle Paul, his fellow believers, and all those aboard ship, and all because GOD had made a promise to Apostle Paul that he would bear witness in Rome.

"Your righteousness is like the highest mountains, your justice like the great deep. You, Lord, preserve both people and animals."- Psalm 36:6
(NIV)

GOD's righteousness is like the highest mountains, GOD's faithfulness stretches to His throne in Heaven. That is the good news. GOD will fulfill His purposes and promises to Christians. The bad news is that GOD will also make good on His warnings to unbelievers.

"Whoever believes in the Son has eternal life, but whoever rejects the Son will not see life, for God's wrath remains on them."- John 3:36
(NIV)

The above story of the deliverance of Apostle Paul and other passengers was a wonderful illustration of the salvation which GOD offers to all who believe in Him. The majority of those on board ship trusted in their instinct- themselves, in their captain, and in their ship to get them safely to their destination. The gentle south winds at Fair Havens proved deceptive. They were not as safe as they thought to reach their destination. At first they supposed they would be able to weather the storm, but in time, they lost all hope. They could do nothing to save themselves. There was one man on board ship who promised salvation if they would do as he said – Apostle Paul. In so doing, all were saved from disaster and brought safely to shore.

> *"I have told you these things, so that in me you may have peace. In this world you will have trouble. But take heart! I have overcome the world."* - John 16:33 (NIV)

Someone reading this book- Pastor's corner might be overwhelmed with the storms of life, and you realize that you are hopeless and helpless. There is only one person who can save us, and His name is Jesus. He died for sinners, and GOD raised Him from the dead. He offers salvation to all those who will trust in Him. Those who seek to abandon Jesus for some lifeboat will only perish. Those who trust in Him will be delivered safely, as those on board that ship had to entrust themselves to Apostle Paul, so we must entrust ourselves to Jesus Christ. He is our only means of deliverance.

CHAPTER THIRTY-TWO:
THE LORD SHALL CHANGE YOUR STORY

"What then shall we say to these things? If God is for us, who can be against us?"- Romans 8:31 (NIV).

When I was growing up in Ibadan, West Africa, I grew up with color erased from all around me and with so much love and trust. In many part of the world, how you are perceived is already decided before birth. The color of your skin, the texture of your hair, accent of your tongues, the city and country you are born in, and what your last name is. All of these things contribute to how you will be labeled in this modern society. It determines what opportunities you will be presented with as opposed to ones you will have to work for, or even the ones that will always be out of reach.

It was conditioned to the society that Latinos are unsuccessful, dumb, and ghetto. And that African-Americans are lazy, dumb, dangerous, and ghetto. And that Asians are weird and eccentric.

'There is neither Jew nor Gentile, neither slave nor free, nor is there male and female, for you are all one in Christ Jesus."- Galatians 3:28 (NIV).

I remember taking a corporate leadership class in pursuit of doctoral degree at one of the regional universities in the United States. At the beginning of the semester, one of the lecturers stated that there is racial achievement gap in his course- referred to the grade disparities between various ethnic groups. It manifested that among students, African Americans and Latinos were more likely to receive lower grades. His statement challenged me, with my tight schedule having a full time career as a computer professional, full time ministry as a Parish Pastor, PhD student and family responsibilities. I strived to study harder and got a grade of A (Excellent) in that class. Later, I remember telling the lecturer that hard work is the key to educational and eventually occupational attainment not stereotype threat that can negatively affects performance as a result of self-handicapping tendencies through activation of salient racial stereotypes.

"While Jesus was in one of the towns, a man came along who was covered with leprosy.[a] When he saw Jesus, he fell with his face to the ground and begged him, "Lord, if you are willing, you can make me clean." - Luke 5:12 (NIV).

Let's imagine a man in his mid-thirties. He has just started out in life. He has a beautiful wife and two adorable little children, with a third one on the way. One day, he comes home from work and shows his wife and the children small sores in his hand. He takes it easy at work for a couple of days, but the sore just keeps getting bigger and bigger, but it still doesn't hurt. After a few days however, they are alarmed, and his wife persuaded him to see a physician who is trained in the area of skin infections.

For two weeks, the sore gets bigger and bigger, until it almost covers his whole hand. It becomes white around the edges. It doesn't cause much pain, but it sure looks horrible. At the end of two weeks, the physician says to this younger man, **"I have diagnosis on your ailment. I am sorry to inform you that you have leprosy. You are going to have** *to leave your family, home, job, and go off to live with the other lepers out behind the town."*

Hearing this, the man was terrified. It is a death sentence. His family would come and bring him food every day. But they couldn't get close. They would leave the food at a certain place on a rock and when they withdrew, he would go pick it up and eat it. In this way, he watched his children grow up, yet was never able to touch them. He watched his wife cry as she left the food, but he was never able to comfort her.

"Jesus reached out his hand and touched the man. "I am willing," he said. *"Be clean!"* And immediately the leprosy left him."- Luke 5:13 (NIV)

According to the Jewish law, if a person touched someone who was unclean, they became unclean also. So why did Jesus do this? Jesus Christ did it for the sake of the leper. Christ never heals anybody just to show others that He can heal. Christ never heals anybody to gain public fame. No, Jesus simply wanted to show love to the leper. Jesus Christ was not scared of his sores, or put off by his rotting flesh. The touch said, *"I am here with you. I sympathize with you when no one else does. I understand. I love you."*

Do you ever feel like a leper? Jesus is saying the same thing to you today that *"I am here with you. I sympathize with you when no one else does. I understand. I love you."* Jesus touched the leper to show him that He loved him.

Do you feel sometimes that people treat you like a leper? Do you feel mistreated? Overlooked or looked down upon? Do what the leper did. Cry out to Jesus Christ today. Stop confessing lies of the society. Confess your faith. Say the same thing GOD says about you.

Let me change the way you think and it will change the way you live. Here are some things the Bible says about you that you need to become, things you should say about yourself:

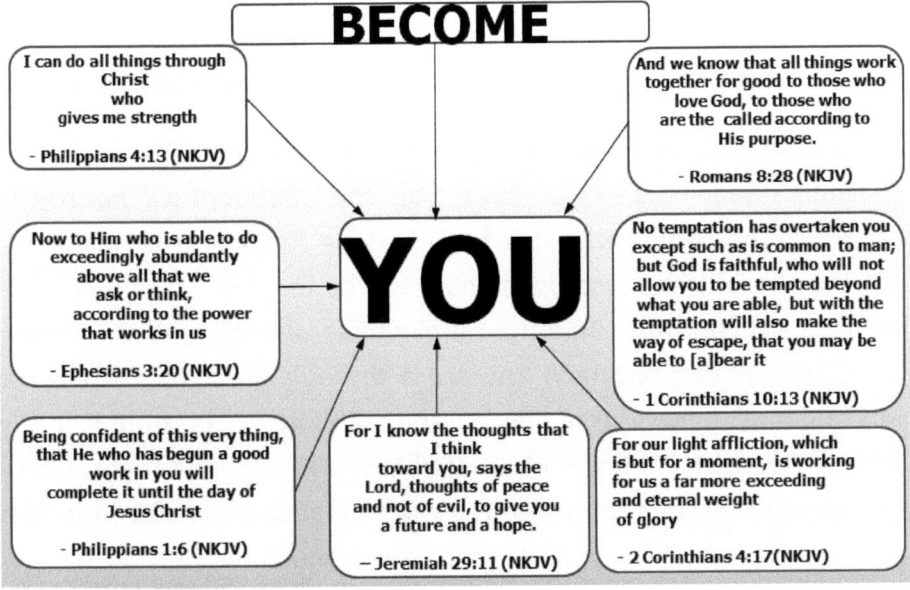

The Bible says in Romans 2:11, NKJV (paraphrase) —"**For there is no partiality with God.**" GOD does not show partiality or favoritism and neither should we. Jesus Christ put an end to this, destroying the dividing wall of hostility. All forms of racism, prejudice, and discrimination are insults to the work of our Lord Jesus Christ on the Cross of Calvary.

Another thing is that there is only one race—the human race. Africans, Asians, Caucasians, Indians, Arabs, and Jews are not different races. Rather, we have different ethnicities of the human race. All human beings have the same physical characteristics (with minor variations depending on DNA composition and environmental factor). More importantly, all human beings are equally created in the image and likeness of GOD. There shouldn't be any room for any sorts of boasting or degrading based on our physical appearances and looks.

You don't have to wait a long time for your life to get better. It can start today, if you decide to do something that you can do right away, change the way you think towards yourself and others. What you think will determine the quality of your life. You're not a victim of circumstances or other people's choices. No matter what, you have the power to create a fulfilling life for yourself by changing the direction of your thoughts.

The Bible says in Isaiah 33:24 (NIV)- **"And the inhabitant will not say, "I am sick"**; The people who dwell in it will be forgiven their iniquity."; and the sins of those who dwell there will be forgiven". Do you understand this verse? You come from a bloodline of Light and you live for GOD. You are not ordinary! You are a thoroughbred. Your lineage is why you must believe from now on, though there will be trouble in the world but you shall be victorious, darkness will disappear right before you, sickness will flee from you, you will be made ten times better than previous years, and you will be made a thousand times more by the end of this year. The Lord shall change your story. Get ready for it. I see you with joy unspeakable and a shout for hallelujah in Jesus' Name. Amen.

Chapter Thirty-Three: Good Days Are Ahead of You

"And God is able to bless you abundantly, so that in all things at all times, having all that you need, you will abound in every good work."
- 2 Corinthians 9:8 (NIV)

I woke up with above scripture vibrating within my spirit. I knew GOD wanted to bring out something from it. As I was performing my early morning walk meditating on the scripture, my attention was drawn to a property that's listed for sale. I approached a middle age woman in the front of the house and introduced myself as one of the neighbors. I asked her why they want to sell their beautiful property, her look appeared as if she has been beaten down, and her shaking response was divorce.

Life will always have seasons where we are hard pressed on every side. Yet in the crushing moments, GOD's all-surpassing grace will prevail. GOD release His grace to encourages, empowers and sustain us in the time of adversity. You might have been beaten down like our neighbor, you might have been thinking about your mistakes. I want you to know that GOD didn't create you to destroy you. You are not GOD's experiment; you are created to excel in any situation you found yourself.

"I said, 'You are "gods"; you are all sons of the Most High."- Psalm 82:6 (NIV).

Nothing you have done has cancelled your destiny. Learn to let go of yesterday, you just need to learn from the past mistakes and focus on today for the betterment of tomorrow. In spite of those circumstances, the grace of GOD is available to still become who GOD has created you to be. You just need to give up to GOD. It is never too late to start over. Your best day is ahead of you. You can be greater than yesterday. You can still fulfill your destiny. We can count on GOD to take care of everything we need, in every circumstance of life, all the time.

The Bible says in Psalm 8:3, NIV- **"When I consider your heavens, the work of your fingers, the moon and the stars, which you have set in place"**. As I was meditating, and consider the magnitude of the universe, the beautiful flowers and morning sweet bird singing. I exclaimed in amazement, and then I asked GOD, my daddy how do you do these?

"Woe to those who quarrel with their Maker, those who are nothing but potsherds among the potsherds on the ground. Does the clay say to the potter, 'What are you making?' Does your work say, 'The potter has no hands'?" – Isaiah 45:9 (NIV).

Just as our minds cannot comprehend the magnitude and complexity of the universe, it cannot comprehend the magnitude and complexity of GOD's love for us. Obviously, GOD is far greater and more powerful than the universe He created.

The most important thing I have learned in my life journey is that our world is truly created from the inside out. Our thoughts, feelings and beliefs determine the experiences that are delivered to us. Losers will build around their lives their weaknesses but over comers build their lives around their strengths. You need to motivate yourself. Learn to visualize good days that are ahead of you. You need to build your life around your strength and try to work on your weaknesses.

"For I know the plans I have for you," declares the LORD, *"plans to prosper you and not to harm you, plans to give you hope and a future"*. – Jeremiah 29:11 (NIV)

If you don't want to cut corners, the journey to greatness might be long and difficult. Prior to the time I became a Church Pastor, my wife and I as a young couple had to wake up in the middle of the night to pray together. There was a day she was tired and I was upset because she couldn't pay attention while praying together. And she reacted and said **"sometimes you have to do it without me, many times you have to face GOD alone"**. Her statements changed my prayer life and strengthened me to study my Bible.

"David was greatly distressed because the men were talking of stoning hlm; each one was bitter in spirit because of his sons and daughters. But David found strength in the LORD his God."- 1 Samuel 30:6 (NIV).

You need sustained motivation to walk it. Otherwise, there is no way you can go through the years of hard effort needed. You can't depend on others to keep on pushing you every day. You need to motivate yourself. You need to inspire yourself. Don't wait for someone to praise and motivate you. Ninety percent of time, circumstances mightn't be encouraging. You just need to develop a thick skin. You need to encourage yourself until those negatives turn to positive outlooks.

The Bible says in Ephesians 6:6, NIV -"**Obey them not only to win their favor when their eye is on you, but as slaves of Christ, doing the will of God from your heart.**" The problems arise in the journey of a Christian when he is trying to do like someone else. Instead, you should try to add a little more to what is expected.

Let me share this testimony with you. There was a day I was praying to GOD, and I was asking GOD to make me like some of the greatest men of GOD. As I was mentioning their names, GOD was responding by asking me, *"Is that all"*. Later, I asked the Holy Spirit why GOD the Father was responding to me in that way. The Holy Spirit then told me that there are many better gifts and anointing in Heaven that has not been released yet to any humans. GOD wants me to be unique.

Contentment and fulfillment will never come when you are trying to be exactly like others. You are created uniquely.

Keep yourself inspire and do not associate with negative people, places or things. Some will encourage you, some will discourage you. Some will make you to doubt your calling or purpose and some will support you through thick and thin. Negative people or things can dry you up until you become as pessimistic as they are. Remain focus and good days are ahead of you.

Chapter Thirty-Four:
You Are Taking Over in Jesus' Name

"Those who are wise will shine like the brightness of the heavens, and those who lead many to righteousness, like the stars for ever and ever"- Daniel 12:3 (NIV)

Have you ever watched a movie where the star is seemingly in eminent peril? No matter how real the movie may look, one thing is sure the star that plays the hero will never be defeated. Just like those movies, the Bible likens believers to be like stars. You are a star that will never be defeated by the enemy. In fact, not only will you not lose you will win every single time.

The Bible says in 2 Corinthians 4:8, NIV:

"We are hard pressed on every side, but not crushed; perplexed, but not in despair."

Those attacks on you, your family, health, ministry or finances may be intense right now but I have good news for you that you will never be defeated. You will take over the gates of your enemies in Jesus' name. So why are you afraid?

The Bible says in Hebrews 13:6, NIV:

"The Lord is my helper; I will not be afraid. What can mere mortals do to me?"

Without your cooperation, no demons can touch you, nobody can limit or stop you, nobody can defeat you, nobody can do anything to you because the GOD that cares for sparrow and lilies in the field is watching over you.

GOD boldly declared in Isaiah 54:17, NIV:

"no weapon forged against you will prevail, and you will refute every tongue that accuses you. This is the heritage of the servants of the Lord, and this is their vindication from me," declares the Lord."

This is our inheritance as Children of the most High GOD. That should make someone to be rejoicing and peaceful today. That inheritance is given to us on the basis of our faith and relationship with the Lord Jesus Christ, the Son of GOD.

The Bible says in Colossians 2:15, NIV - *"And having disarmed the powers and authorities, he made a public spectacle of them, triumphing over them by the cross."* Each time I follow my children to play and have fun with basketball games; I always want their team to win. No loving father ever wants his child to lose. Likewise, GOD our Heavenly Father wants us to win every day, and to enjoy life abundantly. May be you just are not sure whether GOD approves of people enjoying their lives daily; take a look at John 10:10, NIV:

" The thief comes only to steal and kill and destroy; I have come that they may have life, and have it to the full."

This is an absolutely amazing scripture because it clearly tells us that GOD doesn't just want us to be alive, but GOD wants us to be victorious and enjoy being alive. GOD wants you and me to live with joy – abundant, overflowing joy with smiling face. Enemy has no weapons that will work against us if our relationship with GOD is intact.

The Bible says 1 John 4:10, NIV -**_"This is love: not that we loved God, but that he loved us and sent his Son as an atoning sacrifice for our sins."_** GOD sent His only begotten Son with the knowledge that His Son would have to die for our sins. Can you even begin to imagine how much GOD loves you? His willingness to send His only begotten Son for the forgiveness of our sins proves it. GOD sent Jesus Christ so that we would be victorious over sin, death and the grave.

Jesus Christ was put to death in the flesh but made alive in the spirit because it impossible that He should be held in the grips of death. Jesus never sinned; His spirit remained alive, even though He suffered death in the flesh. Death cannot truly occur to a Spirit Being like Jesus. The grave has no power over sinless flesh and that is why if you genuinely give your life to Jesus Christ you will be raised to eternal life because His righteousness is accounted to those who believe in Him.

"I lift up my eyes to the mountains— where does my help come from? My help comes from the Lord, the Maker of heaven and earth."- Psalm 121:1-2 (NIV)

One of the most successful military strategies an enemy can employ in warfare is to separate you from your supply lines, to keep you from receiving reinforcements or supplies. That's exactly what the devil wants to do when he has you, your family, ministry, job, marriage, finances and health under attack, enemy wants to separate you from your main supply line which is GOD, and to keep you from receiving reinforcements and orders from our spiritual headquarters in Heaven. The only way the enemy can spiritually terrorize you is by living in sins, doubt, separation and isolation from GOD's Word and His Church.

When you find yourself under spiritual attack, you need to understand that conflict or battle with lucifer (satan) is spiritual, and therefore no tangible weapons can be effectively employed against him and his demons. You need to effectively put on GOD's armor (Ephesians 6:10-18). Putting on GOD's armor will bring victory because it is far more than a protective covering. It is the very life of Jesus Christ Himself.

> *"Rather, clothe yourselves with the Lord Jesus Christ, and do not think about how to gratify the desires of the flesh."* -Romans 13:14 (NIV).

When you do, He becomes your hiding place and your shelter in the storm, just as He was to David. Hidden in Him, you can count on His victory, for He not only covers you as a shield, He also fills you with His life.

GOD's armor is the name of Jesus. The Bible says in Philippians 2:10, NIV

> *" that at the name of Jesus every knee should bow, in heaven and on earth and under the earth,"*

Jesus' Name is so powerful and exalted, there is only one other name that even comes close to it. It is the first great name ever made known to man. It is the holy and unspeakable name of the Father GOD Himself. That is the awesome name GOD revealed to Moses when He spoke to him from the burning bush and told him to deliver the children of Israel out of the bondage of Egypt. When Moses asked what he should say when the Israelites asked the name of the GOD who had sent him, GOD answered: *"I AM THAT I AM"*.

GOD's armor is the Blood of Jesus. The Bible says

> *"This is my blood of the[a] covenant, which is poured out for many for the forgiveness of sins."*- Mat. 26:28 (NIV)

The Blood of Jesus is so powerful because it is the union of the human nature and the Divine nature in one person of Jesus Christ. Even though the Blood of Jesus was human blood, it drew its efficacy from the Divine nature with which the human nature was united to be the man called Jesus Christ. The very fact that GOD raised Jesus up is evidence that GOD accepted His precious and powerful Blood for the remission of sins and deliverance of mankind. No wonder GOD says in Exodus 12:13, NIV:

"The blood will be a sign for you on the houses where you are, and when I see the blood, I will pass over you. No destructive plague will touch you when I strike Egypt."

GOD's amour is the Word of GOD. The Bible says in Hebrews 4:12-13, NIV:

"For the word of God is alive and active. Sharper than any double-edged sword, it penetrates even to dividing soul and spirit, joints and marrow; it judges the thoughts and attitudes of the heart. Nothing in all creation is hidden from God's sight. Everything is uncovered and laid bare before the eyes of him to whom we must give account."

The GOD's word is a living entity. The sharp sword of GOD's Word heals completely where it wounds and gives life where there is no life. Your tactical advantage in the battle of life is your personal relationship with the Holy Spirit and your reliance on the Word of GOD.

I want you to know that you are a winner in the game of life. You are taking over the gates of your enemies. GOD is giving you victory today over the current situation you find yourself. Rejoice, you will completely take control over your situation in Jesus' name. Amen. Hallelujah!!!

Chapter Thirty-Five:
GOD Is Able To Keep You From Falling

"To him who is able to keep you from stumbling and to present you before his glorious presence without fault and with great joy" - Jude 1:24 (NIV)

GOD is the Mighty GOD, the Creator and upholder of all things; GOD is every way qualified to keep us, He is able because He has all the power in Heaven and on earth; instances of person as in the life of Abram prove that GOD is able to present us before His glorious presence without fault and with an exceedingly great joy.

"As he was about to enter Egypt, he said to his wife Sarai, "I know what a beautiful woman you are. When the Egyptians see you, they will say, 'This is his wife.' Then they will kill me but will let you live. Say you are my sister, so that I will be treated well for your sake and my life will be spared because of you."- Genesis 12:11-13 (NIV)

Few months ago, I was in a conversation with a friend that reached out to me from England. We were sharing our Christian experiences, journey of faith and benefits of having good Christian mentors. We agreed that faith can fail, faith does fail; at least, honestly, my faith does.

The incident in Abram's life described in above passage should give an encouraging word today and one that is desperately needed by those whose faith is failing. GOD is able to keep you from stumbling and the river of joy shall spring up again in your life.

True faith in GOD is a faith that grows. In my Christian walk with the Lord, I realized that the Lord permits certain events in our lives to grow our faith. Each daily event seems different and unique. For Abram, the first event was that of a famine.

"Now there was a famine in the land, and Abram went down to Egypt to live there for a while because the famine was severe" - Genesis 12:10 (NIV)

As an immature saint, Abram had no idea that suffering and trials were a part of GOD's curriculum in the school of faith. While Abram believed in GOD, he knew little of GOD and what He is capable of doing in totality. Abram may have thought that the GOD who has called him was not able to control nature. From where I grew up in West Africa, the traditional worshippers or pagans have different gods ranging from the gods of thunder, water, iron and other deities that are distant objects of worship, and they do not personally interact with men. In the pagan insight, these 'gods' had various limited powers.

At a point in the life of Abram, perhaps he thought that GOD should not be bothered with matters like rain or crops. It never seemed to occur to Abram that GOD was not only greater than the famine, but the giver of it, as a test of faith.

"Jesus looked at them and said, "With man this is impossible, but with God all things are possible."- Mathew 19:26 (NIV)

Egypt seemed to be the logical solution. Abram did not consult GOD, but acted independently. No altars were built in Egypt to our knowledge, nor are we told that Abram ever called on the name of the Lord there. His request of Sarai also reflects his spiritual condition. It would thus be safe to say that Abram's faith failed in the face of that famine.

"Say you are my sister, so that I will be treated well for your sake and my life will be spared because of you." – Genesis 12:13 (NIV)

It seems that Abram made his decision to go to Egypt without considering the consequences. Just outside the border of Egypt, Abram began to contemplate the dangers which lay ahead. It really was an ingenious plan.

Such a plan was evil for several reasons. First of all, it tended to ignore the presence and power of GOD in Abram's life.

GOD had promised the ends, but seemingly He was unable to provide the means. He promised a land, a seed, and a blessing. Now it seemed as though Abram was left to his own devices to procure them.

The Bible says in Psalm 38:6-8, NIV - ***"I am bowed down and brought very low; all day long I go about mourning. My back is filled with searing pain; there is no health in my body. I am feeble and utterly crushed; I groan in anguish of heart."***

Like Abram like David. Can you imagine, David a man after GOD's heart? He slumped in hopelessness, he was troubled, he couldn't understand why he was suddenly cast down so low. This man hungered for the Lord, pouring out his heart daily in prayer. He revered GOD's word, writing psalms that extolled GOD's glory. But now, in his depressed state, all he could do was to cry, telling GOD that he was at the end of his rope. And he had no idea what could happen and why he was going through those events in his life.

I had a privilege of my mother visited my family from Africa; at the dinner table my wife and I were sharing some of the events that happened many years ago when we relocated to the United States. There was a night that we were walking side by side on the street, held our hands together, praying and weeping because we didn't know what the future holds in the United States.

"So do not fear, for I am with you; do not be dismayed, for I am your God. I will strengthen you and help you; I will uphold you with my righteous right hand."- Isaiah 41:10 (NIV)

Like many discouraged Christians this day, David tried to figure out why he felt so empty and broken in spirit. He probably relived every failure, sin and foolish deed in his life. At some point he must have thought, Oh, Lord, have all my reckless acts left me so wounded that I'm beyond hope?

Just like David, none of us is immune from the attack of the spirit of discouragement. But GOD has given us power and authority over all demonic attacks and needed strength to overcome all undesirables' events.

"I have given you authority to trample on snakes and scorpions and to overcome all the power of the enemy; nothing will harm you."- Luke 10:19 (NIV)

Discouraging spirit comes straight from the bowels of hell. And the time comes when every dedicated believer is overwhelmed by this sudden and unexpected experience. No Christian brings it on himself, nor does the Lord send it. Such an attack usually has nothing to do with any specific sin or failing by the believer.

"I am the vine; you are the branches. If you remain in me and I in you, you will bear much fruit; apart from me you can do nothing"- John 15:5 (NIV)

GOD permits those situations in our lives to increase our faith, to demonstrate His Power, for us to know His Power, and to develop our total dependence on Him alone.

The Bible says in Psalm 34:19, NIV – *"The righteous person may have many troubles, but the LORD delivers him from them all"*.

Can you imagine the lonely, agonizing nights Abram must have spent, wondering what was going on in the palace with his wife and Pharaoh? Abram had asked Sarai to lie so that it would go well with him. And it did go well.

> *"He treated Abram well for her sake, and Abram acquired sheep and cattle, male and female donkeys, male and female servants, and camels."* - Genesis 12:16 (NIV)

Pharaoh sent many gifts to Abram and treated him royally. The only thing which kept Abram from enjoying his treatment was the realization of what it meant. Pharaoh was giving these things to Abram as a dowry. It did go well with Abram, without Sarai, his wife. Prosperity is never a blessing without the peace which can only come from being right with GOD.

Abram was in a tight situation, he was allowed to fail and to flounder until his situation was seemingly hopeless. We are not told that he cried to GOD for help.

> *"As a father has compassion on his children, so the Lord has compassion on those who fear him"* - Psalm 103:13 (NIV)

GOD intervened in the life of Abram. Pharaoh and his household were struck by some kind of plague.

> *"But the Lord inflicted serious diseases on Pharaoh and his household because of Abram's wife Sarai."* - Genesis 12:17 (NIV)

While in Egypt, Sarai's purity was protected and Abram's life was preserved. More than this, all of his possessions were kept intact. And to top it off, Abram and those with him were escorted back to the land of Canaan.

The principle of GOD's faithfulness in the face of our failure and adversity is one that applies to us this day as well:

> *"if we are faithless, he remains faithful, for he cannot disown himself."* – 2 Timothy 2:13 (NIV)

Our faith, like Abram's may fail. But the blessed truth of GOD's Word is that when our faith fails, GOD doesn't.

Abram chose to doubt GOD's presence and power in the face of a famine. His actions were those which showed he was willing to sacrifice principle for self-preservation. In spite of Abram's failure of faith, GOD preserved him and even prospered him. Ultimately, GOD brought Abram to the place that he should have been.

Abram did not reject GOD; he simply failed to believe that GOD was able or willing to act on his behalf. Just as He saved Abram in spite of himself; he can save us too regardless of the situation we find ourselves right now. He can also sanctify us in spite of ourselves. Our eternal security, our salvation, deliverance and sanctification rests in His faithfulness, not ours.

Chapter Thirty-Six: Let GOD be your treasure

"The house of the righteous contains great treasure, but the income of the wicked brings ruin."- Proverb 15:6 (NIV)

I want you to know that as you will respond to the call of GOD today you will hear from heaven and enter into GOD's purpose for your life. There are those who have entered the very chambers of His holiness and touched the heart of GOD. They have walked with Him (Gen 5:24, paraphrase), talked with Him (Exo 19:19, paraphrase) and heard His voice (Gen 15:1, paraphrase). Some have even spoken with Him *"face to face"* (Exo 33:11, paraphrase). They were changed men, never again the same. Today, the Lord shall give you a lifetime experience in Jesus' Name.

The Bible says in Isaiah 45:3, NIV - *"I will give you hidden treasures, riches stored in secret places, so that you may know that I am the Lord, the God of Israel, who summons you by name."* The treasures from GOD are not to the mighty or the strong, but to those who will seek Him with their hearts. GOD is looking for those who will not be satisfied with the material blessing, but will ever long for the inner courts of the Most High. He seek someone like King David, who will determine in his hearts *"I will not enter my house or go to my bed, I will allow no sleep to my eyes or slumber to my eyelids, till I find a place for the Lord, a dwelling for the Mighty One of Jacob"* (Psalm 132:3-5, NIV).

GOD is constantly seeking for those that fear and love Him genuinely.

"For the eyes of the LORD range throughout the earth to strengthen those whose hearts are fully committed to him. You have done a foolish thing, and from now on you will be at war" -2 Chronicles 16:9 (NIV)

GOD is searching for those who will heed the call to draw near and not delay (Psalm 53:2, paraphrase). GOD told the sons of Zadok, who kept the sanctuary, that their ministry to Him would be their inheritance. He said that they were not to be given any possession in Israel, for *"I am their possession"* (Ezekiel 44:28, paraphrase). This was a special service, for they ministered to GOD. It is difficult for us to understand that GOD should require the ministry of a man. But we have been made in His image, with the capacity for fellowship with Him.

"But the Levitical priests, who are descendants of Zadok and who guarded my sanctuary when the Israelites went astray from me, are to come near to minister before me; they are to stand before me to offer sacrifices of fat and blood, declares the Sovereign Lord. They alone are to enter my sanctuary; they alone are to come near my table to minister before me and serve me as guards."- Ezekiel 44:15-16 (NIV)

The Bible says in Job 22:24, KJV - *"Then shalt thou lay up gold as dust, and the gold of Ophir as the stones of the brooks."* Despite the fact that GOD created everything, there is one thing that remains unchanged, GOD desire to see our loyal hearts eager to know Him more and more daily. GOD searches today for those who will make Him their single desire, who will say with David that *"the Lord is the portion of mine inheritance"* (Psalm 16:5, paraphrase). They will be His special possession, for *"the Lord hath chosen Jacob unto Himself, and Israel for His peculiar treasure"* (Psalm 135:4, paraphrase) Jesus told His disciples to *"sell all"* for *"a treasure in the heavens that faileth not ... for where your treasure is, there will you heart be also"* (Luke 12:33 -34, paraphrase). Those who find GOD as their treasure will be a treasure unto Him: *"And they shall be Mine, saith the Lord of hosts, in that day when I make up My jewels"* (Malachi 3:17). *"And the Lord their GOD shall save them in that day as the flock of His people: for they shall be as the stones of a crown, lifted up as an emblem upon His land"* (Zechariah 9:16).

There is no more treasure under the heaven than GOD. When we make GOD our treasure we get the prospects of wonderful blessings that we have never dreamt before. GOD is an eternal treasure that cannot be spent or lost. If we spend as much time and efforts seeking GOD as we used to spend seeking material wealth, then we will get a priceless treasure. This will give us more real and exciting blessings than we can imagine. We are living in a complex world with different scary dangerous news. If we make GOD and His word our highest priority. It will help us not to lose faith and not to fall into a state of murmuring. Are you ready to make GOD your treasure today?

Chapter Thirty-Seven: You Shall Rise Again

"Being confident of this, that he who began a good work in you will carry it on to completion until the day of Christ Jesus."
- Philippians 1:6 (NIV)

When we receive Jesus Christ as our personal Savior, GOD begins to work in us. Nobody is born fully grown, so GOD has to build our Christian character. In other words, when we are saved, GOD begins a good work in us to perfect us because it's not right to take the children's food and throw it to the dogs. We are not a finished product yet. GOD will build a true Christian character in us through different ways, but the first things first. Some people try to develop character, but they have no true foundation. And that foundation is Jesus Christ you must genuinely receive Jesus Christ.

The Bible says in Romans 5:3-4, NIV- *"Not only so, but we[a] also glory in our sufferings, because we know that suffering produces perseverance; perseverance, character; and character, hope."* GOD allows pressure to come along our path. GOD wants the oil of gladness and the wine of joy in our character. He wants that which will sustain and give strength, but the only way that GOD will get it out of us is to press it out. Are you going through challenges of life right now? Are you having trouble? Are you feeling pressure? Don't look at them as obstacles;

start looking at them as opportunities! These are the things that GOD allowed to build our true character; catalyst in fulfillment of our destiny.

Everyone living on earth is going to pass through a duration of trial and tribulation whether you're a Christian or not, but you have control over the manner in which you respond. A child of GOD must strive to trust GOD totally through the trial and tribulation- read the Bible; it's important to bring your feelings before GOD in prayer all times; You must remember that the first thing that Paul and Silas did in the midst of the tribulation they encountered was to glorify and worship GOD- put on some praise and worship music and sing to the Lord; Count your blessings, you have to look back to see how GOD has affected your lives.

The Bible says in John 11: 23, NIV – *"**Jesus said to her, "Your brother will rise again."**"* Lazarus has been dead for four days meaning the process of decomposition had to take place. According to John Chapter 11 (paraphrase), the first person to meet our Lord Jesus Christ as He came close to Bethany was Martha. She was overcome with grief at the loss of her beloved brother.

*""**Lord," Martha said to Jesus, "if you had been here, my brother would not have died. But I know that even now God will give you whatever you ask."**– John 11: 21-22 (NIV)*

Her response was not a rebuke of His delay, but a testimony of her trust in His healing power. Therefore, He said unto her, Martha, **" Your brother shall rise again!"**

When it seems that all is lost, when you feel that the knot is unraveling in your hand, when you feel that the end has come and there is no more hope. Just like Martha, when Jesus Christ the Son of GOD comes on the scene with the greatest message of hope that we could ever hear. Therefore, it does not matter what the circumstances say, or what other people think, or what impossibilities lay ahead, ***"You Shall Rise Again."***

When your family is on the brink of destruction, I have good news for you – You shall rise again! When your capital has been depleted, and the vision appears dead – You shall rise again! When you have been laid off from your work - You shall rise again! When you feel depressed, despondent, and hopeless due to circumstances beyond your control – You shall rise again! When your ministry is about to be destroyed or has been destroyed by the host of hell - You shall rise again!

When the medical report is unfavorable and not too good at all, I want you to believe in a healer – Jesus Christ. We find no record in the gospels that Jesus Christ did not turn away anyone who came to him for healing, nor do we find that any disease was too difficult for him to heal. He even raised the dead. Miraculous healings still occur today— evidence that Christ is still our Healer. The Purpose of Divine Healing is to Glorify Jesus Christ.

"Jesus said to her, "I am the resurrection and the life. The one who believes in me will live, even though they die; and whoever lives by believing in me will never die. Do you believe this?" – John 11: 25-26 (NIV)

Jesus Christ revealed Himself in a deeper fashion to Martha. Martha, I AM the Resurrection and Life. Martha did not realize the power, the glory, and the sovereign majesty of the person who stood before her that day. Don't start accusing Martha wrongly because most of us do not understand the efficacy and effectiveness of the Power of GOD that lives within us as the children of GOD.

For Jesus Christ is the I AM that I AM. He is GOD, the Creator of all things, the sustainer of all things. He is the I AM of the Old Testament and King of Kings of the New Testament.

He is the Resurrection Power. He is the Glory and Majesty. He is GOD Almighty. The person that stood before Martha that day and He is the same one that is knocking at the door of your heart and life this today, telling you that - You shall rise again!

The Bible says in 2 Timothy 2:3, NKJV- **"You therefore must endure[a] hardship as a good soldier of Jesus Christ."** The Africa Elders says that **"no matter how dark the sky may be , there will be some traces of light"**. No matter what you're going through right now, I want to assure you that there's a light at the end of the tunnel and it may seem hard to get to the light but you can do it , just keep focusing and holding on to GOD.

Think about GOD in every situation - He is the First and the Last, the Beginning and the End! He is the keeper of Creation and the Creator of all! He is the Architect of the universe and the Manager of all times. He lives in eternity- He always was, He always is, and He always will be. He cannot die. He is all powerful. He is unmovable, unchangeable, undefeated, and never undone. Herod couldn't kill Him, The Pharisees couldn't confuse Him, people couldn't hold Him! Nero couldn't crush Him, Hitler couldn't silence Him, Scientists and this modernization can never replace Him.

GOD is light, He is good and kind. He loves you more than you can imagine. In His Mercy, He will see you through that situation you find yourself in Jesus' name.

I pray that every plan of enemies over your life, health, marriage and ministry will be scattered by the host of heavens and that our Heavenly Father will preserve you. You shall make it to the end in the Mighty Name of Jesus. Amen.

Prayer Points

1. Father GOD, let the Blood of the Lamb, the Blood of Jesus Christ cleanse me from my sins and impurities in the Mighty Name of Jesus.

2. Father GOD, open my understanding in the name of Jesus.

3. Father GOD, bring to light to everything planned against me, and my family in the name of Jesus

4. Father GOD, make my life, family and this nation a citadel of holiness, wonder, miracle, power and glory in the name of Jesus.

5. Father GOD, let every veil preventing me from having deep spiritual vision be removed in the name of Jesus

6. Father GOD, let every satanic joy over my life be terminated permanently in the name of Jesus

7. Father GOD, let every spirit of barrenness disappear in the name of Jesus.

8. Father GOD, terminate every curse of barrenness in our midst in the name of Jesus

9. Father GOD, let every monthly monitoring of my womb of joy by evil ones be terminated in the name of Jesus

10. Father GOD, let every spiritual poison introduced into my body in any forms disappear in the name of Jesus.

11. Father GOD, let there be uncommon miracles in my life and family today in the name of Jesus.

12. Father GOD, today terminate every evil covenants and satanic appointments in my life in the name of Jesus

13. Father GOD, manifest to destroy the works of evil in every areas of my life in the name of Jesus

14. Father GOD, show yourself mightily in my situation in the name of Jesus

15. Father GOD, let satan be rebuke today in the name of Jesus.

16. Father GOD, repair everything that has been damaged in my life in the name of Jesus.

17. Father GOD, let a new thing spring up in my life in the name of Jesus.

18. Father GOD, let every door that's open to the evil ones, be closed in the name of Jesus.

19. Father GOD, every door that I have opened to the devil be closed forever in the name of Jesus.

20. Father GOD, I release my body, soul and spirit into your hand, cleanse me by your name in the name of Jesus.

21. Father GOD, let all filthy garments be removed from my life in the name of Jesus.

22. Father GOD, in this season, let your mercy rest upon me and my house hold in the name of Jesus.

23. Father GOD, you are my strength and my shield; you are my hope, refuge and strength. Father, uphold me with your righteous hand in the name of Jesus.

24. Father GOD, in this season, let every calamities and famine be removed completely in the name of Jesus.

25. Father GOD, in this season, show and prove yourself mightily in my life, family, and career/business in the name of Jesus.

26. Father GOD, let the seasons of affliction, poverty, sickness, warfare, ignorance, persecution and carnal desire be over in my life and our local churches in the name of Jesus.

27. Father GOD, release your power into my life and let my enemies be fragmented, be confused and flee before me and my family in the name of Jesus.

28. Father GOD, do not allow the death of your son, Jesus Christ to be in vain in my life in the name of Jesus.

29. Father GOD, today repair every damage tissues in my body in the name of Jesus.

30. Father GOD, glorify your name in all my circumstances in the name of Jesus

31. Father GOD, let the Blood of Jesus avail for me. I release the Blood of Jesus into every areas of my life in the name of Jesus.

32. Father GOD, make a public show of my enemies in the name of Jesus

33. Father GOD, deliver me from the hold of darkness and translate me into your marvelous light in the name of Jesus.

34. Father GOD, before the end of this year, let me be released into the land of honor in the name of Jesus.

35. Father GOD, disgrace every power that want me to labor in vain in the name of Jesus.

36. Father GOD, don't let me come to this world in vain; let me fulfill my purpose in the name of Jesus.

37. Father GOD, let every activities of destroyers be terminated in the name of Jesus.

38. Father GOD, let this year be the year of abundant joy and uncommon breakthrough for me and my family in the name of Jesus.

39. Father GOD, let every darkness around my spiritual life be removed in the name of Jesus.

40. Father GOD, remove death completely from our midst in the name of Jesus.

41. Father GOD, I thank you for another wonderful day. I thank you for influencing my priorities, provisions, for pardon of every sin and for protections from evil work in the name of Jesus.

42. Father GOD, I thank you for guiding me away from temptation and any trap planned by evil ones to destroy my life, family, the children and my ministry, Father GOD destroy those plans in the name of Jesus

43. Father GOD, I thank you for Divine and angelic protection. In this season, rebuke completely any devourer that rises up against my life and blessing in the name of Jesus.

44. Father GOD, you are Jehovah-Jireh, my provider. I thank you for everything I have. I thank you for everything in my future will come from you. Thank you for bringing the provisions I need for the remaining part of this year and my tomorrow in the name of Jesus.

45. Father GOD, I thank you for accelerating my progress in the name of Jesus.

46. Father GOD, use this season to complete and perfect work in my life and my family in the name of Jesus.

47. Father GOD, I thank you for answer my prayers in the name of Jesus.

48. Father GOD, let every weeping ends today in the name of Jesus.

49. Father GOD, all my goodness swimming in the ocean of life, be restored back to me in Jesus' Name.

50. Father GOD, every evil ones militating against my blessing be bound in the name of Jesus

51. Father GOD, let this year release my breakthroughs in the name of Jesus

52. Father GOD, I shall not die but live in the name of Jesus.

53. Father GOD, let your mercy and protection be upon everyone in my family in the name of Jesus.

54. Father GOD, make me and my family to please you in the name of Jesus

55. Father GOD, release anointing and power to prosper under any condition into my life in the name of Jesus.

56. Father GOD, go before me today in the name of Jesus.

57. Father GOD, anything that will not glorify you in my life and family, let it be removed in the name of Jesus.

58. Father GOD, I thank you for answer my prayers and giving me victory in the name of Jesus

59. Father GOD, let me be perfect in the name of Jesus

60. Father GOD, move my family forward by your power in the name of Jesus

61. Father GOD, do a new thing in our midst in Jesus' Name.

62. Shalom, surround us with your Peace in the name of Jesus

63. Father GOD, let every battle around be over in the name of Jesus

64. Father GOD, surround me with your miracles and wonder as from now in the Mighty Name of Jesus.

65. Father EL-HYM, change my name to reflect your glory.

66. Father GOD, let me get to my divine destination on time in the name of Jesus.

67. Father GOD, let your protection rest upon your people all over the world in the Mighty Name of Jesus.

68. Father GOD, increase me mightily and never to go backward anymore in the Mighty Name of Jesus.

69. Father GOD, let me make it to the end in the name of Jesus.

70. Father GOD, thank you for answer to these prayers in Jesus' Name. Amen

ACKNOWLEDGEMENTS

All glory belongs to GOD Almighty that makes this possible. I can never be grateful enough for all the people that GOD had brought into my life and across my life over the years and the way He used them to encourage me, enrich me and to fulfil GOD's plan for my life. I am very thankful to my wife, Olayemi. She has grown to my closest friend and adviser. Without her GOD-given insight, it would not be possible to write this book.

I am very thankful for my GOD's given children- Mobolawa, Akinkunmi and Olakanmi. I owe a very special word of thanks to my parents- Elder Isaac Olabode Adio (Of-blessed-memory) and Deaconess Janet Bolawa Adio and to my sisters- Toyin, Tayo, Teju and Doyin who have loved me over the years unconditionally. I am also thankful to my brother-in-law, Dr. Oyeniyi Owoade for his encouragement and support.

I do want to thank those who have contributed greatly to who I am in Christ today including but not limited to my grandaunt Prophetess Nihinlola Adesina (Of-blessed-memory) and others. Also, I am thankful to the special people that encouraged me to write this book – Pastor Daniel Ajayi Adeniran, Pastor James Fadel and Pastor Stephen Rathod for his prayers. I am also indebted to our beloved church members at the Jesus Is Alive World Center who had supported me and believed in GOD's vision in me. You are all wonderful. Finally, I want to thank the staff of Stellar Literary Press and Media for their assistance on this book.

You can contact Pastor Isaiah Adio at the following address:
        129 Kensington Blvd,
        Blandon, PA 19510.

Biography

Pastor Isaiah Adio is a loving, dedicated, and compassionate leader with a sincere desire to serve the Lord Jesus Christ and the Body of Christ. He joined The Redeemed Christian Church of God, miraculously in 1995 at The Redeemed Christian Church of God, Ladipo Oluwole Parish, Ikeja, after the Holy Spirit brought to him the map and direction to the church. He is a citizen of the United States of Nigerian descent and has been living in the United States with his family for more than 20 years.

Pastor Isaiah Adio was ordained by General Overseer, Pastor E.A Adeboye, his spiritual father and mentor. He has faithfully served the Church in many capacities before he was called by GOD to start the Parish as a Pastor in October 2008 at The Redeemed Christian Church of God (Jesus Is Alive World Center), Quakertown, Pennsylvania, and now located in Reading, Pennsylvania.

Pastor Isaiah Adio is a bi-vocational pastor. His academic background includes a Bachelor's Degree in Computer Science. A Master's Degree in Information Systems from the Minot State University, Minot, North Dakota, USA completed in 2012 and the Doctor of Business Administration (DBA in view), California Southern University, Costa Mesa, California, and many other professional certifications. By GOD's grace, he has achieved a successful professional career, including but not limited to the position of Director of Information Technology and IT Chief position in private and government sectors.

Pastor Isaiah Adio is committed to the expository (verse-by-verse) teaching and preaching of GOD's Word with an emphasis on practical application. He earnestly desires to see every member of the local church actively involved in ministry. GOD has used him to plant many churches as a Lead Pastor. He believes that GOD is more than able to do big things in small places.

He has consistently written a weekly teaching and prophetic series called "Pastor's Corner" since 2009. It has been a source of encouragement and blessing to many lives.

He believes so much in the power of prayer. One of his favorite verses in Mathew 19:26, NIV —*"**Jesus looked at them and said, "With man this is impossible, but with God all things are possible."*** His teaching shines through in his messages each and every week as he clearly delivers real-life applications of GOD's Word in his messages. His style is bold and sincere. He believes whole-heartedly in the power of the Word of GOD and the ability to uplift and guide the children of GOD through all phases of life.

By the grace of GOD, he is married to Olayemi Adio. GOD has blessed them with wonderful, gracious, and lovely children- Mobolawa, Akinkunmi, and Olakanmi.

Pray for Pastor Isaiah Adio as he serves the Lord that the Lord Jesus Christ will continue to encourage him and enable him to end well in Jesus' Name. Amen.

Printed by Libri Plureos GmbH in Hamburg, Germany